REFORMATION ESSAYS

REFORMATION ESSAYS

by

J. P. WHITNEY, D.D., D.C.L.

Published for the Church Historical Society

LONDON
SOCIETY FOR PROMOTING
CHRISTIAN KNOWLEDGE

First published 1939

MADE IN GREAT BRITAIN

PREFACE

Of these Essays some have been printed before: Essay I in *London Theological Studies*: University of London Press, 1912. Essay II in the *English Historical Review* (1920). Much of Essays III and IV appeared in my Hulsean Lectures for 1910. Essay V was in the *Cambridge Historical Journal* (1932). I should like to add here that "Erasmus" was the special subject for the Lightfoot Scholarship when I was awarded it in 1882, and he has, so to speak, been a friend of mine ever since; I read the Letters first in the Leyden edition, and to pass, in later years, to Mr. P. S. Allen's edition, with its immense learning in the notes, was a great delight.

I am indebted to the various authorities concerned, for making no objection to the reprinting. Essay II is reprinted by permission of the Editor and Messrs. Longmans, Green & Co. Ltd.

Since I began to put these pages together, memories of my teachers and pupils seemed to crowd upon me, and so many of them have passed from us, that I feel as if I were on sacred ground.

I must not close this preface without acknowledging the great help given me by a former pupil of mine, while she was at Newnham, now teaching in the South Hampstead High School : without her help my labours would have been much greater and the delay in publication longer. I must also thank the staff of the S.P.C.K. and the printers.

J. P. WHITNEY.

Epiphany-tide, 1939.

1169

CONTENTS

ESSAY I

CONTINUITY THROUGHOUT THE REFORMATION

B

SYNOPSIS

CONTINUITY THROUGHOUT THE REFORMATION

THE study of history both in its method and in its matter has undergone great changes. In its method greater stress is laid now upon "origins" and upon the tracing out of gradual growths: sudden revolutions, social upheavals, meteoric personalities, are more rarely assumed, and, when they are said to be found, the statement only leads us to distrust our guides. Natural Science has taught us to look for the gradual work of lesser agencies, for the earthworm with its fourteen years of patient work, rather than for the plough with its compressed energy of a single day. We are told that the human system always holds within itself the germs of many diseases which are only held at bay by the power of resistance, and that, when some subtle cause lessens that power, the waiting germs make themselves effectively felt. Any age or any crisis may in much the same way be held in solution, as it were, in the age which precedes it. To understand the one we must know the other.

And again, as Lord Acton has pointed out, the accumulation of historic material has made the work of the modern historian more difficult, and given him fresh responsibilities. With the presence of new witnesses to be cross-examined, with a more stringent law of evidence, old verdicts must be revised, and old prejudices put aside. When this has been done, passions that have been built up with age will lose their foundations, although the essential principles are left behind.

In most fields of historic study this twofold task has been either wrought roughly to an end or else been much more than well begun. But when we come to the Reformation we find a gulf, unbridged and untunnelled, separating critical scholars and the multitude of the unlearned. Nowhere has the gathering of materials, national, political, economic, theological, liturgical, and biographical, been more extensive or more manysided. And yet when leaving that inner, and too often secluded, room in which the scholars work, we pass into the general reading-room of the inquiring public, we find old verdicts still repeated with an unshaken confidence, old prejudices still at their strongest and their worst.

It would be too much, of course, to expect that even the scholars themselves should be at one: it is much if they are even at peace amid their differences among themselves. A few of them may still keep a violence of expression or an intolerance of mind that should belong only to intellects less trained and passions less controlled. But there has been naturally a great improvement, and that in spite of some lapses in taste. The marvellous scholarship and accurate knowledge of Denifle make us regret more deeply the anger which disfigures his great posthumous work upon Luther and Lutheranism, and it would be easy to take examples of the same failing from the other side, since sides there must be. Yet after all there has been a great advance. Thus although the Papacy has often been treated with an admiration too blind or a hatred too fierce, even here there is substantial agreement between, for instance, Creighton and Pastor; each reaches to impartiality and balance, even if the one seems to do it more through his knowledge of the world, and the other through his command of research. And to speak of those manuals which are more summary and bibliographical, we are able to pass from the Catholic Funk to the Protestant Moeller (revised by Kawerau) without much disturbance.

It is easy to see why there has been imperfect filtration from the level of scholars to the level of the ordinary reader. The Reformation has its Napoleonic legends of many

4

different Napoleons in one camp or another. And these legends must be handled delicately lest they should perish, and weaken Empires by their fall. Because the Reformation saw the beginnings of many systems and policies that separate us to-day, we are too apt to assume sudden creative forces at its birth, to ascribe finality to its judgments. Romanist, Anglican, Lutheran, Protestant of all kinds are all guilty in this way, although they may label the forces differently or choose different judgments for approval.

We may also neglect continuity or again forget the axiom that history should be studied always as a process, not as a picture; and we thus often hide the true view of the Reformation. It has been studied, for instance, too much in detail, in single scenes, apart from its continuity as a whole. Thus in English history it has been too much the fashion to take the reign of Henry VIII apart: as a result some threads of interest have seemed to hang quite loosely, the significance of some things has been lost, and incidentally surprise has been caused that the king, reforming so far, did not reform much further. In German history in the same way the period up to 1529 has drawn so much notice to itself that the significant features of the later history are obscured: the activity of Melanchthon, the Concord of Wittenberg, the many attempts at union among Protestants, the significant labours of Gropper, Pflug and the other "mediating" theologians, the preparations for a Council, and the negotiations at Trent, the activity of the Jesuit Canisius at the court of Ferdinand I: all these are essential parts of the history, and the more critical earlier years are easily misunderstood if these are left out of account. We gain but an imperfect view of a man and his character from a study of one crisis in his life: in the same way movements must be studied as a whole, and the history of Lutheranism—to take one instance—is only made intelligible by a study of the later sixteenth century. English religious history suffers from the same restricted view. Puritanism, for instance, is a continuous development of one factor in the earlier Reformation: from Tindal through Hooper and Cartwright to the Millenary petition is an unbroken history; on the other hand, the school of Laud represents an earlier school that had been dominant under Henry VIII. When we give these later days their true place in the history, the whole becomes consistent: like the spires of Wren's city churches, isolated periods blend together, and we understand each separate one the better for its fellows. The true lower limit of the Reformation period for the Continent falls somewhere about 1648, for England about 1660.

But it is even more necessary to begin our study of the Reformation by understanding the Middle Ages. We still sometimes hear medieval used as roughly equivalent to dark and ignorant; the beauty of the Franciscan ideal, the glory of medieval architecture, are held to be things strangely out of keeping with their surroundings, odd manifestations like a hardened criminal's love for his mother. Too often the Reformation is summed up as an attack upon medieval abuses: this is a double injustice—it is unjust to the Reformation, for it ignores the positive side of the movement; it is unjust to the Middle Ages, for in practice it seems to assume their principal activity to have been the production of abuses. We gain a truer view of the case if we regard the Reformation as the outcome of the Middle Ages, not merely as a matter of chronology but of spiritual descent. And there is one great gain from the study of "origins." We start, often unconsciously, with the ideas of our own times; we view the past from our own standpoint; we see too plainly the lie of the roads that lead to us, the trend of the watershed that slopes towards us; there are other roads that would appear just as plainly from another standpoint, but them we cannot see; there are streams and valleys that are hidden from our sight. Our standpoint fixes the details for our view; we become more self-centred; our own ideas are driven more firmly into our being. We miss the larger

6

revelation that comes from a study of a larger world, the revelation of a purpose wider than our own. But when we study "origins" everything is different: we must see side by side the pregnant possibilities which have made ourselves on the one hand, and, on the other hand, have formed people very different from ourselves; we retrace the path of the ages, and we learn many things as we come to know the road. This process brings with it a state of mind very different from that which dwells mainly in the present, one which is calmer and more scientific. There is between the two states of mind something of the difference that there is between the thinker who studies the electrical theory of matter and the highly trained electrical engineer; the latter seems for the moment much nearer the actual world of life, but the former in reality does much more for the eventual growth of science and the progress of mankind. To look closely at origins lets fresh oxygen into the heated chamber of present discussions. The study of early Gaul, for instance, has done something to allay animosity between German and French scholars; the study of early Germanic institutions has done something to bring together the ardent democrat and the stubborn monarchist. To him who seeks the truth first of all there is always added something that he did not seek. This is the great advantage in studying origins, and when we stand beside the cradle from which great principles have grown, we learn to distinguish them from the passions in which we have clothed them.

If any age needs to be studied in this way it is the age of the Reformation; and yet not only the popular taste, but even more serious study, has mainly chosen other methods. It is well to be reminded (as we are by Dr. Kidd in the preface to his excellent *Documents illustrative of the Continental Reformation*) that "origins are common ground. Developments mark the points of divergence." Differences, therefore, are best studied in that common ground, and not in their more crystallised form. To do this is not—and this truth must be emphasised—to ignore principles or to mini-mise them. It is rather to study principles where their real importance, their substance apart from their accidents, is best to be understood. No historian has done more for the Reformation period than Maurenbrecher, and he was always searching for origins in the history of thought; the delimita-tion of principles, it sounds a truism to say it, is best done on the border-line itself; diplomatists in official capitals are apt to grasp too largely or to yield too lightly. Where our period has been studied in this way, the results have been most fruitful. In the preparation for the period too, how much is to be learnt from the history of local efforts at reformation: from a better knowledge of "reformers before the Reformation"; from the history of the great Councils; from the study of the influences moulding various reformers. What a new light is thrown upon later issues when we see the future Cardinal Pole approaching Melanchthon in his views of justification, or find Caraffa, the future Paul IV, in his earlier years, a practical reformer of the Erasmian type. To know men before they diverged is often to grasp the secret of their divergencies. Hence it is needful for the sake of understanding the Reformation to study its origins in the Middle Ages and to look at its characters not where they diverged most widely, but at moments when they ap-proached most closely.

Centuries seem to vary in their energies as well as in their aims. Thus the thirteenth century is the greatest of medie-val centuries, great in its characters, in its institutions, in its movements. After its glow and rich variety the fourteenth century may seem dull and drab. But that, too, has its move-ments of beginning life; the Papal Schism leads to new dis-cussions of ecclesiastical polity, just as the strife between Emperor and Pope had led to discussions of Sovereignty, and of Church and State. When great questions such as these were raised, thought was stimulated and the fresh theories which were formulated became in their turn ground for new discussion. Thus thought gained a new vigour and a fresh variety before the Middle Ages closed—a vigour which was specially felt in the Universities, above all at Paris. This tradition of thought was handed down to the later Gallicans, connected on the side of politics with the French monarchy, on the side of learning with a long line of illustrious scholars.

If we were to confine our attention to France, the transition from the Middle Ages to the age of Louis XIV seems gradual and smooth; there is little internal response to the external thunderstorm caused by the clash of Papal claims and Protestant individualism. It is true France did show herself alive to the charm of the Renaissance, and of that movement with its influence more might be said. Here it is enough to say that the Renaissance should be regarded as a movement within the Middle Ages, not as an accidental disturbance from outside. It had begun before the taking of Constantinople by the Turks in 1453; Greek had been taught in Europe before that date and had found many devotees; men who lived after its "abolition" now began to long for its restoration. Bessarion, the future Cardinal, with his much-noticed beard, represented the Eastern Church at the Council of Florence (1439), and by his continued sojourn in the West became one of the many channels along which Greek culture spread. The flight of scholars from Constantinople to Europe was less important than the scattering of manuscripts that followed the fall of New Rome, but neither of them caused, even if they did slightly quicken, the movement which in many ways recalled the other and earlier Renaissance of the thirteenth century.

A sign of the new life which stirred the world in the Renaissance is to be seen in the many monastic or semi-monastic revivals of the fifteenth and early sixteenth centuries. Again and again monastic reformers had revived the old ideal and founded new orders or strengthened the old; then again and again the impulse had died away and a fresh

9

reform had been needed. The process was unbroken, and in the series the reorganisàtion of the Lower Saxon Benedictines by John Busch takes its place. The Augustinian Friars followed with a reform of a deeply spiritual type, the movement that gave us Staupitz and influenced Luther. A little later Italy felt the same impulse to monastic reform, spreading with a closer grasp of the Renaissance and of practical life into the Theatines of Caraffa—afterwards Paul IV. If Spain only later felt the impulse, it produced in the Society of the Jesuits an example whose success has claimed them from the medieval for the modern world. Here, too, we have a continuous history which bears throughout the same impress, medieval in its type. Ximenes, even earlier, falls into its line.

But more striking still is the history of the Brethren of the Common Life (1380). They were semi-monastic, for they lived a common life even if they were not monks; their work was practical and thoroughly Christian in tone, education was one great part of it, and from them the Renaissance in Germany seems to have inherited this characteristic. Their schools spread from the Netherlands into north-west Germany, and wherever they went they carried the love of the classics, a taste for copying manuscripts, and a special devotion to St. Jerome. Under these brethren Erasmus began his education. His earlier letters, which England can now study either in the fine Latin edition of Dr. P. S. Allen, whose irreplaceable loss we so lately mourn, or the excellent English of Mr. Nichols, make it plain that before he knew Colet he had devoted himself to "sound learning," and had already taken St. Jerome for his model. By "sound learning" he meant that solid theology, founded upon the Bible and the Fathers, upon which he placed his hopes for the world and the Church. Had this been encouraged always, abuses could not have grown up so readily and so widely: in its encouragement by his own generation he saw the best path to a possible reformation. His letters to his early friends (notably to Cornelius, with his triple *alias*) show that under these earlier influences Erasmus had learnt what true theology was, and how, as with St. Jerome, theology and scholarship could be united. Critics to-day may doubt—as Erasmus himself, perhaps, doubted at times—what was his exact share in the Reformation. But there can be no doubt that any history of it would be incomplete which did not take in his work. Such a history, however, might, on the other hand, begin with him and do so with but little sacrifice of completeness.

And yet a history of medieval thought and scholarship, which only looked backwards and left the Reformation altogether out of sight, might well take him as a type of what the thoroughly medieval Brethren of the Common Life aimed at in their education. Hence in the case of Erasmus—so often called (possibly with an undue depreciation of Aeneas Sylvius) the first of the moderns—it is easy to bridge over the gap between two distinct periods. It may be worth while to come back later to his "modernity." But if the modern world may claim him, so surely may the medieval.

The personality of Luther has always seemed to the common man easy to understand, and to the scholar hard to explain. Wherein lay the secret of his power? "What made Luther" Lord Acton thought to be an enigma not yet fitly answered. Behind his vigorous manhood lay the peasant life of the countryside and the burgher life of the town, two things that passed with changes gradual and small from the fourteenth to the sixteenth centuries. There was also another part of his background a little more modern in its colouring—that outburst of German University life reaching from the foundation of Erfurt (1392) to that of Wittenberg (1502). Erfurt from the first was marked by its devotion to Biblical studies, never wholly neglected in Universities but enforced from time to time, as when Grosseteste at Oxford ordered the first morning lecture to be on the Bible. Wittenberg was the great home of Renaissance learning with its new and daring research. The one University made Luther, and the other he helped to make. The life of the peasantry, of the city and of the University were varied parts in the background of his life, and along with them mingled the earnestness, the deep personal piety, that marked the Augustinian revival. But backgrounds and influences do not, of course, wholly explain a man, either in his life or in his influence.

Since the appearance of Denifle's work upon Luther, controversy has been busy. The bitterness of theological prejudices—always sensitive with the sensitiveness that knows itself not quite in the right, and must therefore cloak prejudices as principles—has been keen; we have been carried backwards into other days more robust (may we call it?) in their methods. But it has also been pleasant to see how scholars have passed behind the smoke of battle to mark out exactly what ground has been gained or lost. The most solid part of Denifle's work is his treatment of "justification," and by his continuous exposition of it from the writings of medieval theologians one thing is certainly proved. It will be remembered how Luther describes the joy he felt upon reaching the true explanation of "the righteousness" or "justice of God" (Rom. i. 17). He had believed, so he said, that the justice meant God's "active justice," that by which he judged mankind, but suddenly it flashed upon him that the "justice" was the "passive justice" by which God attributed His own righteousness to mankind. By this revelation he was lifted from despair to joy. But Denifle has shown that this interpretation so far from being novel was traditional; that Luther himself must have known this earlier exegesis, and had indeed given it in his lectures upon Romans delivered before, according to his later narrative, the new light had dawned upon him. There is no need to suppose intentional deceit, for change of interests produces inexactness. It is never easy to retrace one's mental growth, and natures such as Luther's always find it hard to be either just or exact in descriptions of their former mental states. "Confessions," even if poured forth by a St. Augustine, are given to exaggeration, to shades too dark and contrasts too sharp.

But the special truth which stands out, and which must be admitted in any future estimates of Luther, is that here, where his cardinal doctrine of "justification by faith" was concerned, he was more medieval than we are apt to think. To put it in other words, the break in the history of doctrine was not even in the case of Luther so abrupt as has been thought. The medieval treatment of the doctrine contained, in germ if we like, many possible growths; there were many elements in it, and by alteration of the emphasis laid upon any one of these, a different result might be gained. Ritschl's masterly treatment of the medieval theologians has illustrated the existence of these diverse elements. Denifle has shown the exact medieval teaching in one essential matter where the break between it and Luther was formerly held to be most abrupt. The new light which changed the life of Luther had really shone throughout the ages of darkness. So far as this one matter was concerned, there was, then, no great revolution, although there was a change in proportion and a shifting of emphasis. For there were different elements in the medieval doctrine, and the omission of any one of these would naturally alter the proportions or even the nature of the whole. Thus Gardiner found fault with Cranmer not for the emphasis he placed upon "faith" but for his neglect of "charity."

It is significant to notice the direction in which a difference between Luther's and the medieval teaching must be sought, and may be found. The medieval doctrine always kept in view the fact that life was lived within the Church, that the processes of salvation were not purely individual. It was within the sphere of corporate life that salvation was to be wrought and gained. With Luther, on the other hand, the individual was chiefly thought of, and the process was personal, mainly or even altogether; it was the sinner's conviction of his salvation which really was his salvation. A man stood face to face with God, and in the intensity of that personal and individual meeting, the corporate life, as the sphere of faith, seemed to lose its former importance. This element had not been lacking in the older view, but it had been qualified and modified by the other element of the corporate life. In the same way Luther's attack on Indulgences was made in the interest of the individual life, which in this respect was being sacrificed to the supposed interests of the corporate body. So, too, that refusal to accept Papal authority to which he was gradually pushed in the Leipzig Disputation was an assertion of individual freedom. Prierias had said (and Eck agreed with him) that the Pope was the Church, and that what the Pope sanctioned must be right: against this Luther asserted the claims of conscience. The whole tendency of medieval thought, indeed, everywhere and in everything was to place the society above the individual, the school above its isolated member. The tendency changed and with it changed much else.

From this leading fact of medieval life there arises the great difficulty in discussing medieval authorship. No man thought or wrote for himself: he preferred to take the very words of other authors and he held himself perfectly at liberty to do so. The continuous chronicle built up by life after life, handed on from generation to generation, was the type of medieval work. Even the *Imitatio Christi* is a composite work, and it is most probable that Thomas à Kempis was rather editor or even scribe than author, for whom we must probably look to Italy. Such a writer merged himself in the band of other writers who had worked before, and he was ready to lose himself in the line of those who came after. From something of the same cause come the many difficulties which meet the student of Wyclif. It is very difficult to say how much "editing" his English works may

14

have undergone: indications of different dates exist side by side in the same work, and the same difficulty appears, although to a lesser degree, in the Latin works. Outside Wyclif's own work, too, there was a more popular Lollard literature shaped and reshaped and then shaped again, about which it is difficult to say anything as to authorship: individual writers were merged in the school, and at last—to take the crowning example which Loserth has shown us— Hus copied word for word, save with the substitution of Bohemia for Anglia, long passages of Wyclif's work. There was no law of copyright in the Middle Ages, and men liked to repeat ideas in the very phrase of their original expression. There are, again, medieval works, such as the *Prick of Conscience*, ascribed to Rolle of Hampole, which have no personal touch, and where the personal note is altogether wanting. One must not expect to find the rights of ownership written plainly on the surface or even revealed beneath it. The ascription to a special writer, even the fact that a work may be claimed for him, makes little difference. It is easy to prove the absence of such evidence of ownership, but it is not possible to go further and state that because of its absence the claim to authorship understood in the medieval sense is unfounded. There is, just because of their method, an elusiveness about medieval writers which makes investigation into authorship often very difficult, and indeed almost useless. There is little of the individual, there is much of the school, to be found in the work. This is so, simply because the individual was little thought of, and thought little of himself, while the school was always placed above him. It is a commonplace that this preference for the society above the individual shows itself in every part of medieval life, political and economic, as well as religious.

But in modern times all is changed. The individual now bulks more largely: he is even apt sometimes to take his projection upon the Brocken of his age as giving his real dimensions. But the change—which is seen very clearly in the realm of art—has its gain as well as its loss. The individual misses something of discipline, the world loses something of coherency, but there is a gain in variety and personal energy. In Art, for instance, the earlier Italian medieval painters (as Mr. Grant Allen has so well shown in his *Evolution of Italian Art*), dealing with sacred scenes such as the "Annunciation" or the marriage traditions of the Virgin's family, had reproduced the same characters much in the same situations: they looked at the pictures of their forerunners as types which they must follow closely; departures from traditional treatment crept in only in the backgrounds, such as those in a beautiful inset landscape of Lorenzo di Credi. At length we come to later days when painters relied more upon themselves, and gave their individual tastes larger scope in composition and selection. Apart from the natural growth in technical skill we gain in variety and richness of thought, although there is a loss, probably inevitable with the growth of Art, in religious sympathy and reverence. But the marked change in Art as the Middle Ages come to an end illustrates the general change which is also found elsewhere.

In this emergence of the individual, then, lay the great secret, the great power of the sixteenth century. Its great men are those who show individual power by a revolt against the force of society, not as in some other ages by their support or leadership of society. Years of a many-sided education in the discipline of a many-sided corporate life had done its work, and the individual was sometimes educated enough, sometimes merely thought himself educated enough, to take his place as an individual, not merely as a member of a society. Side by side with the ready acceptance of a corporate life there had been frequent murmurings against its restrictions, or its occasional tyranny. The medieval heretic had made his protest, but he was for the most part of little significance for the history of thought, as the great medieval thinkers (with the striking exception of Marsilius) were rather on the side of society and of system. But as the break-up of the Middle Ages drew near these murmurings had become louder and commoner. They are heard, perhaps, most of all in the field of economics: the manor, the guild, give place—although but gradually—to individuals in competition, and to the recognised sovereignty of the slowly-shaped national State. Old customs, old privileges, little by little lose their force. Money-rents, a wage-earning class, long growths of distant beginning, become fixed parts of social and economic arrangements. All these are regulated by barter and bargain, by the play of individual wishes and interests rather than by the older rules of corporate life and corporate interests. The history of Usury and of the controversies about it is significant. The Revolt of the Peasants in England (1381), the long-delayed Peasants' War in Germany (1524) are parts of the general process. A general rise of a new nobility, the growth of a richer merchant class, are both part of the same movement. There was a general impatience of old restraints; there was a new feeling of individual power, a longing to risk individual actions and to further individual interests. For reasons of this kind, too, the monastic life had begun to lose its attraction. Founders of monasteries were rarer, and inmates of monasteries were fewer. This result was, of course, intensified by the corruptions which were to be found in some cases, by the comparative uselessness of a monastic life compared with its activity in earlier days, and by the loss of a sufficiently high ideal, testified to even by the frequent attempts at reform already mentioned.

Towards the close of the Middle Ages there was, then, an outburst of individualism. We have lately learned what boundless energy works in the motion of the tiny atoms of a body apparently at rest, and what manifestation of energy results from the disturbance of their equilibrium. Something of the same kind happened with medieval society: its individual parts seemed released from coherence, and there was almost at once a great display of individual energy. There was, therefore, power to be utilised, but there was also power that might be misused. There was a need of instruction and guidance, and thus fresh responsibility was placed on those who ought to give them. At the very time when the Church and its leaders were suffering from past neglects and present defects, a new and pressing responsibility was brought upon it and them. It was this which made the real crisis of the Reformation. It was the mishandling of the crisis which made the tragedy.

In this individualism is to be found that which separates the medieval from the modern world. We may return for a moment to the common description of Erasmus as the first of the moderns. This is true so far as his way of looking at things and his wit is concerned, with the one qualification mentioned above, that Aeneas Sylvius (Pius II) was almost as modern in his humour. In Erasmus there is an openness about himself and his feelings, almost a display of himself: the personal touch transfigures everything: he goes his own way and he judges everything from his own point of view. He laughs at himself, at his weaknesses and his adventures, he expects others to laugh with him and to be interested in him. A truly medieval writer would never expect others to be interested in him for himself: he would enlarge instead upon his monastery or his civic home. Erasmus is always, first and foremost, an individual, and even strives to be a personality. It is here that his modern spirit is to be found. The absence or the presence of the individual element is something of a test by which we distinguish between medieval and modern times.

But it is true, on the other hand, that both Erasmus and Luther give us an unfavourable description of the system under which they were brought up. In the case of Erasmus his letters to his early friends serve to correct the impression made by some later and longer passages of description.

There are few writers but could find faults in their schools, or at any rate in the methods of education followed there. When Erasmus, moreover, spoke of the system that had produced him, he was either trying to raise the tone of education, or else he was making out a case for himself; he was dealing with his facts more as a literary man than as an historian. But it is clear that in spite of faults easy to find, and of mistakes easy to see, the teachers among the Brethren of the Common Life had something at any rate of a great ideal; they did aim, although possibly with some deviation, at a sound classical and theological education. The somewhat dark picture Erasmus draws, when it is his object to draw a dark picture, has to be combined with others if we would have the absolute truth.

Something the same is the case when Luther, in his later years, turns to describe his own past. Here, again, Denifle's argument supplies some needed corrections. Luther, in writing nearer to the years he depicted, had spoken more favourably of his own monastic training. When in later years he looked at that past life through the smoke and dust of many controversies, some arising out of the monastic life and vows, he deepened the shades and dwelt only upon the darker features. At any rate the figure of Staupitz with his real halo of piety, the traditions of Erfurt with its Biblical studies, remain untouched, and the impression they give us is confirmed by Luther's own earlier words. In leaving Erfurt, what he felt most deeply was having to give back the "little red Testament" lent to him as to all Augustinians. The unfavourable words used both by Erasmus and Luther, when they deal with the medieval system under which they began to learn, do not justify the conclusion that they owed little to that system. In both cases the personal equation of the observer is unusually large, and something must be deducted to gain a true observation.

If other links are sought between the Middle Ages and the Reformation, we might turn to the mystic theologians.

They were strong in their reception of individual experiences, strong in their close, personal relations with God. In Rolle of Hampole, to take a typical case, there was no repudiation of the Church system of the time, of the claims of authority, or of the brotherhood of others. These were all accepted as part of the furniture of life. But while many medieval theologians made the individual subordinate to the Church, to be trained and disciplined by it in his individual life, the mystic theologians sometimes placed the individual above the corporate life, sometimes lost sight of the latter altogether. Tauler's sermons had an immense attraction for Luther: the "Deutsche Theologie"—which at first he ascribed not only to Tauler's school, but to Tauler himself—appealed to him with the same force. To Gerson, mystic as well as theologian, he perhaps owed a double debt. It is this assertion of the inner and individual side of religious life which makes so many mystic theologians seem not only out of touch with their day, but almost in rebellion against it; it is in this sense, and in no other, that they can be called "forerunners of the Reformation."

Another outcome of the Middle Ages can only be mentioned here—and that is its political thought. Here, again, the result of closer study has been to show medieval political thought as a really coherent and solid system. Nothing could be more modern than the theories of Marsilio of Padua. The long contests of Pope and Emperor—beginning with the struggle upon Investitures—had raised the question of Church and State, and, in a later phase, of Sovereignty. The limits of ecclesiastical power, both against the State and within the ecclesiastical body itself, were discussed first in the course of the same struggle, and again in the period of the Great Councils of the West. The expression of thought was perhaps sometimes fantastic, but the thought itself was often significant. When Wyclif, for instance, expressed his theory of dominion (borrowed as it was from FitzRalph of Armagh) in the statements that "all dominion was founded in grace," and that "dominion was lost by mortal sin," the doctrine seems strange. It makes all authority, from sovereignty down to the control of land, depend upon personal righteousness, and thus it leads to anarchy. His qualification of the theory by the assertion that "God must submit to the Devil," sounds more fantastic still. But it was meant to limit the theory to ideal conditions, and to say that under present circumstances the best of men must submit to the worst—in a word, that power did not depend upon righteousness but on social facts, and the theory itself was meant to enforce the lesson that for all power and its exercise the holder had to answer before God. To say this was to enforce responsibility, to represent all power as a sacred trust. This truth was as necessary as the form of its expression was fantastic.

It was to speculations such as these that sixteenth-century political thinkers went back as soon as they felt bound to formulate a system. The outstanding fact of their day was the formation of great States with strong Monarchies. The medieval theory of Sovereignty came in usefully here; the medieval theorists had incidentally made large use of Roman law and of classical examples; this use fitted in naturally with the revival of the classical languages. But the freshness of thought in the later age has been over-estimated; for the first half of the century there are few signs of freshness—if we except Machiavelli, a product of politics in Italy where every man strove for himself, and an exponent of the mingled ethics of patriotism and selfishness; only in the latter half of the century do the new conditions of life show themselves in a new freshness of thought. The more the medieval thinkers are studied, the less violent the break appears; Bartolus, as Maitland and Figgis have shown us, bridges over an apparent gulf. The vast body of medieval political literature was not buried out of sight, and one significant link of thought may be noted. Hus in his Latin works largely copied Wyclif, as we noted before. At the crisis of the Leipzig Disputation (1519) a printed volume of Hus's writings was placed in Luther's hands, and thus some of Wyclif's characteristic teaching upon questions between Church and State filtered through to Luther. If in some ways he was ready, or was even forced, to confess himself a Husite, the truer name when we bear everything in mind would seem to have been a Wyclifite. The duty of the State to reform the Church had been a favourite doctrine with the medieval reformer. It was preached more effectively and in a more original way by Luther to the many German princes. There was, further, a large amount of anti-papal literature handed down by the Middle Ages: the *Confutatio Primatus Papae*, probably by the Erfurt Franciscan Matthias Döring and written about 1442–44, is an example; it largely follows Marsilio of Padua and has some links with other works resulting from the Council of Basel—the *Squalores Romanae Curiae*, the *Speculum Aureum*, among them: it discusses and rejects the Wyclifite attack upon clerical property, but it decides strongly against ecclesiastics holding sovereignty— a distinction which carries us back to the celebrated Compromise of Paschal II in the Investiture contest. Döring at Erfurt was one of these writers; others had a centre at Prague; Matthias of Cracow, another of them, died as Bishop of Worms. There was here a tradition which had not wholly died out, and the works themselves remained to be a storehouse for later arguments.

Between medieval and Reformation literature the break is in some other ways not so marked as might be supposed. If we turn to treatises such as the *Loci Communes* of Peter Martyr, or Theodore Beza's *Tractiones Theologicae*, and select one special topic such as marriage and divorce, we find the historical treatment to be medieval in type: precedents of ancient peoples, of Old Testament times, of the later Roman Empire, are collected much as in medieval writers, and it is easy to see that they are held to have a special value as precedents irrespective of their historical setting or of any principle behind them: we might be reading medieval writers. There is nothing of the modern spirit in treating of the past. The same holds good—to take another example—of the earlier writers upon international law. Hugo Grotius in his celebrated work, *De Jure Belli et Pacis*, handles his classical examples, makes his deductions from Imperial Law, in a thoroughly medieval way. One is reminded of the controversy upon the sources of the Nile between Aeneas Sylvius and Gregory of Heimburg, where the question is settled mainly by references to ancient writers. This characteristic of the great work of Grotius is sometimes explained as due to the revival of classical studies, but it is really a characteristic of medieval writers also: parallels from the works of Wyclif or any voluminous medieval writer might easily be found. It is true, of course, that learning became wider and the collected instances therefore more numerous as time went on, but the method of treatment is the same and is essentially medieval.

And yet, on the other hand, there are in these writers features which would often be called modern. The appeal to Scripture is at first sight one of these, but words of Schubert (in his *Outlines of Church History*) state the truth: "What is known as the Scripture principle appeared long before the Reformation—in some cases, as in that of Marsilius, in a very crude form—and the learned Bible studies, which reached their height in the works of Erasmus and Reuchlin, based on a study of the original language and running counter to tradition, were not a product of the Reformation, but a pre-condition of it." This is true although, maybe, a little exaggerated.

A comparison of sixteenth-century with earlier writers shows us not so much a sudden change as a rearrangement of ideas and material, a process spreading over many years and, in the end, giving us something very unlike what was there to begin with. But it takes some time before the change either in style or thought is marked. The earlier Reformers

write in the style of their scholastic predecessors, and the
transition from the scholastic writers is a much more gradual
process than we are apt to assume. Something the same
holds good, too, with more popular literature. The exact
connection between Lollard and early sixteenth-century
tracts has yet to be investigated; there are curious likenesses
which may be nothing more. Tindal has a ring of Purvey,
there is much common to them in disposition, but it is impossible to prove a literary connection. Nevertheless, in
England, Lollard tracts were reprinted and adapted—
especially about the period 1530–60—and the object of re-
issue was to show that the opinions of the Reformers were
not novel. So far were the revolutionists of the age from
wishing to appear revolutionary. But save for the claim, in
some cases only the pretensions, to scholarship there is no
abrupt change as we pass from the tracts of the one age to
those of the other.

The control of Lutheranism soon passed from the theologians to the princes. Zwinglianism—a much more radical
force—had shown itself, but after the second peace of
Kappel (1531) had lost its power; under the seduction of
Philip of Hesse, it had aimed at large political combinations
and had failed. Lutheranism and the Catholic reaction
divided Switzerland between them until the appearance of
Calvinism. Calvin cared little about the practice of States
or the force of tradition: he cared much for what he knew
(as he thought) to be the law of God; he had no doubt about
the right of his Christian Church to legislate and to dictate.
It is needless here to discuss the differences between French
and Scots Calvinism; it is enough to note that Calvin's
theories and legislation have a clearness and consistency
lacking in Luther's. The appeal to Scripture, the appeal to
the individual conscience, become clearer, they are dis-
entangled from the reaction against existing usage which
directed Zwinglianism, and from the submission to the
civil power which dominated Lutheranism. When the first

half of the sixteenth century is over the religious and political situations are clearer.

Up to that time it is easy to see what forces are at work, but it is hard to say what their final effect will be. When we reach the time after the last sessions of the Council of Trent this is easier to foretell. Men and things are settling down, and settling down apart from each other. The earlier years of the century upon which so much stress is often laid are not then those in which the broad lines are permanently laid down. They are followed by a period of interaction, of years in which men modify their views in one direction or another, as did some leading Humanists, and sometimes pass from one roughly marked off group to another group of the same kind. They are years in which permanent division is not a certainty; rearrangement and compromise are in the air. Then, roughly about the year 1570, conditions change, the atmosphere clears, and the divisions, tentatively and hesitatingly formed, become sharply marked, inevitable and apparently permanent. We have finally reached a new age.

The third, not the first, quarter, then, of the sixteenth century is that in which lasting divisions are finally made. In one of his earlier essays, Ranke asserted that until somewhere about 1560–70 there was a possibility of religious unity, that the divisions and separations begun and threatened before that time were not held by men to be irreparable and permanent. And Ranke did not suffer from this assertion as the great scholar Schömann did about an earlier theory of his on the Athenian assemblies. He had changed his mind and come to condemn his earlier belief. But fifty years later he found men still repeating his earlier opinions in spite of his own recantation. Ranke never needed to change his opinion, and all later investigation has shown, as happened often with his trained conjectures, how true and enlightening his opinion was.

Political conditions throughout the century had great effect both for and against unity. Both the imperial and

Habsburg interests demanded internal unity in Germany; and it was needed as much for State as for Church. This had been seen by Charles V, and he had striven to reach it first by the assembly of a council, national if not ecumenical, and then at a later stage (1547) by the use of force. In France much the same was the case. There was much talk of a National Council, which could better remedy abuses and face the menace of Calvinism. Its assembly was urged by Charles de Guise (made Archbishop of Rheims in 1538, and consecrated in 1547). For French interests the hopes from a Gallican Council were many and high, but to the eyes of Pius IV (1559–65) it was likely to lead to a schism. Hence came divergent policies at the French and Papal Courts. All this story has happily (1930) been accurately and excellently sketched by Mr. H. O. Evennett in his most useful work *The Cardinal of Lorraine and the Council of Trent*. So France, like Germany and England, had its own pressing and peculiar problems to solve: but the solutions were not the same from one land to another. Charles V, like Elizabeth of England, had thrust upon him the task of gaining unity and sought to gain it in ways like hers.

The essentials of unity were a reform of abuses and some measure of agreement in doctrine. The latter was the more difficult to bring about, but even here something was done, especially in the discussions which preceded the Diet at Regensburg (April 1541). We may pass over the details, interesting as they are in connection with the history of doctrine, and significant as they are of tendencies easily overlooked. It was possible to take very different views upon the doctrine of justification by faith, around which lay the most formidable of the obstacles to be overcome. There had been many elements in the medieval view, and what was now needed was a broad comprehensive statement combining the varied truths which each theologian saw singly and sometimes alone, a definition aiming at truth by inclusion of whatever was partly true, and not by exclusion of whatever was partly mistaken. This was the task which the mediating school of theologians had set themselves. They could justify themselves by the discussions of the past; their difficulties lay with the present. It was something of the same task which the great Cappadocian Fathers had set themselves in the age after Nicæa, and they approached it somewhat in that patristic spirit.

The general Lutheran view laid stress upon individual salvation, upon the grace of Christ; the risk of this view lay in separating spiritual belief from holiness of life. Upon the other side it was easy to lay stress upon the interests of practical holiness and upon man's own work. If this were done too exclusively the work of Christ might be depreciated, and here was the risk upon that side. Gropper, who prepared the *Liber Ratisbonensis* for a basis of discussion, strongly asserted justification by faith, even by faith alone: the righteousness of Christ was imputed to man, and on this platform he reached a new and inherent righteousness which worked itself out in "charity." The need of divine grace, and the need of a holy life, were thus combined— and this twofold justification became the definition of the mediating Catholics. Both Eck, although he finally signed the definition, and Luther, who was consulted, thought it utterly bad. But the view of Luther was different from that of Melanchthon, who had shaped the definition, and was satisfied with the superior place given to faith over merit. But Luther had by this time become hopeless of unity, and indeed had long been convinced that the Pope was Antichrist. The Legate Contarini represented the reforming Italian school, and he, too, had long been a supporter of Justification by faith; his own views have been variously interpreted but might be reconciled with those of Aquinas. The new definition was, he thought, capable of a Catholic interpretation, and indeed, as with most definitions, much depended upon the prepossessions of those who examined it.

The Consistory at Rome, however, was not satisfied as

easily as Contarini, and the compromise was rejected. At the Council of Trent (Sixth Session, January 1547) the same doctrine was defined in a decree which Harnack calls "a product of art, remarkably well constructed," and which, had it been formulated earlier, might (as he thinks) have prevented the divisions of the Reformation. This decree was shaped largely by the influence of the Jesuits, Lainez and Salmeron; against them Seripando, General of the Augustinian friars, agreed, almost alone, with the Regensburg definition. He represented the Augustinian revival in Germany, which had cleansed the friars of that order, and was really based upon the study of their patron saint. But he found few followers at Trent, where there were many theologians, as Erasmus had thought there to be some twenty years before, more concerned with the approval of what existed and the condemnation of heresies than with the prospects of peace. No sketch, however, of Reformation doctrine—needed as it is for Reformation history—is adequate if it overlooks the work of the "mediating theologians." Their historical significance was great even if their effectiveness was small. But until they had made their attempt and failed, it cannot be said that the issues of the Reformation were clear. Men of their day, at any rate these theologians themselves, were not sure that reforming doctrines, even those upon justification, must lead to a lasting division or would justify its rightfulness. Here again we can only judge truly if we take our stand later on in the century.

If the external history of the Lutherans, and the general sweep of Reformation history suffer from the neglect of the events and tendencies just noticed, it is also true that the internal history suffers likewise. Zwinglians, looking back to a leader who represented the Renaissance and Rationalism; Calvinists, sprung from the French Biblical movement, and the influence of a great systematic theologian; and Lutherans; were at triple discord. The Lutherans always asserted that they had made no break with Catholic doctrine: the attempt to prove this coloured the Confession of Augsburg—the first draft of which was called an Apology, and which Luther spoke of by that name. The object was to make the new departure in doctrine seem as slight as possible. The Zwinglians, upon the other hand, were not disturbed by accusations of a new departure, and the Calvinists—the growing body—relied more on theological system and the Bible than upon agreement with the past. The Augsburg Confession excluded the Zwinglians, and sacramental doctrine threatened permanently to divide the new bodies among themselves. The Wittenberg Concord (1535) was a sign of growing unity; the followers of the Augsburg Confession and the ministers in the Oberland under Bucer (who was restless unless he was engaged in theological diplomacy) drew together, and the process went on. From the side of the State the Augsburg and Leipzig Interims— provisional arrangements of a kind both in worship and doctrine which it was hoped all might accept—had the same intention. The real strength of Melanchthon, too, lay in what is so often held his weakness—namely, his readiness to seek peace and ensue it. There had been (as Humbert points out in *Les Origines de la Théologie Moderne*, an interesting and stimulating work) from the first a difference between him and Luther: he had been an admirer of St. Jerome rather than of St. Augustine, at heart a follower of Erasmus (or at any rate of his own kinsman Reuchlin) as much as of Luther. The debate on the *Adiaphora* was one that would hardly have suggested itself to Luther, and he would never in his later years have been ready with Melanchthon to accept even a limited papal supremacy. The Formula of Concord (1577) was not in itself an ending of strife, for if it bound together many, it shut out all others, and bitter controversies also arose as to its meaning. But it was the end of a long process, during which tendencies towards union and towards distinction had become less confused. After its appearance it was possible to tell more exactly what Lutheranism stood for, and where it stood.

The history which begins with Luther's 95 Theses is only consistent and complete if it is carried up to the Formula of Concord. For that sums up the history of Lutheranism, and it further expresses the fact that Calvinism, "the Reformed" religion, stood over against it. There was, as Lord Acton pointed out, this difference between them: "Lutheranism was governed, not by the spiritual but by the temporal power in agreement with the high conception of the State which Luther derived from the long conflict of the Middle Ages." This gave it a hold upon Germany where the civil power was strong, and the States were many. But "by its lack of independence and flexibility it was unfitted to succeed where governments were hostile, or to make its way by voluntary effort." Politicians utilised and controlled the Reformation movement in Germany much as they tried to do in England, until the school of Laud on the one hand and the Puritans on the other proved too strong for coercion. Then Calvinism, strong in organisation where Lutheranism was weak, arose, and, with the spread of Calvinism in the second half of the sixteenth century, the Reformation took its final course.

But the final shape of the Reformation was moulded as much from the papal side as from the other. Looking at the Papacy solely from the historic side, it represents a purely Western growth. It comes forth from the dim background of early Church organisation as the heir also of Imperial traditions, and as a centre of unity for the barbarian conquerors as they were converted. After the fall of the Empire in the West there comes the long reign of Feudalism—a time in which the Teutonic peoples partly preserved, partly recovered, the spiritual and intellectual heritage of the ancient world. The feudal society as it grew was a framework to protect the ideas of the past; in law and in politics the principles of Roman Law and of Imperialism were thus kept or recovered. There has been in England, since Bryce on the one hand first taught us the permanence of the Empire, and his friend Freeman first taught us on the other hand not to blush for our Teutonic forefathers, a tendency to keep the Roman and the Teutonic elements apart from each other in our minds. But the days of feudalism were the days in which under the solvent power of the social atmosphere they were welded together. The same process was needed, the same process went on, in the Church. We are a little apt to smile at the records of wholesale conversions, whole tribes, whole nations, bowing themselves before the Cross, not always with a clear conviction of what it meant, or what they did. But what happened, at any rate, was this, that they placed themselves under Christianity as a system, as a tutor from whom they were to learn. The centuries that follow from the sixth to the eleventh are those in which their Teutonic ideas and the teaching of Christianity are being welded together. There were dangers in the process; the kings, who sometimes like Chlodwig patronised Christianity, sometimes like Henry III of Germany were devoted to it, were apt to use their great influence for their political or personal ends. There was a danger of the "Germanisation" of Christianity —a danger, that is, of the Germanic States and nobility using its influence for their own secular ends. This was the meaning of the secularising and worldly influences which threatened to transform the Church in the tenth century. In the eleventh century came the reaction; it took the form of a campaign against simony and lay influence—culminating in the struggle upon Investitures: it was an assertion of primitive principles of Church organisation, of the Church's right to self-government, and in a feudal age it took the form of a feudal organisation, although it was able to appeal to earlier precedents of varying value. This was what lay behind the Papacy of Gregory VII; it set up a feudal form of authority in the Church but it was an expression in feudal language of permanent principles. Here we have the feudal stage of Western Christianity; and just as feudalism preserved in politics principles that were of first-rate importance but which without feudalism might have been forgotten, so the feudal stage of Western Christianity preserved for the world the principles of spiritual freedom and Christian unity which without their assertion in a feudalised form might have been completely lost. This is what the medieval Papacy had stood for, with many exaggerations and many mistakes. But what was to happen when the feudal period passed away?

Not all critics of the Papacy and of the abuses which clustered round it had demanded the abolition of the Papacy, or had seen in its destruction an essential of reform. Even Wyclif in his final criticisms of the Papacy, although he held its workings Antichristian, would have preferred a local headship for the Church, although not of necessity fixed at Rome—since he held that there was no reason for the choice of that special seat. But the holder of this headship must be a spiritually minded man, a true successor of St. Peter in life and character. This conception of the Papacy was something like that put forth in the days of the Councils, with their talk of reformation in head and members alike. At Constance, where the forces of Nationalism met the discredited upholders of a divided Papacy, the three theories of a Papacy governed by the Imperial power, of a Papacy really governing the Church, and of a limited Papacy administering with a Council, all found supporters. The result of the Councils was small whether in curbing the Papacy or in furthering reform, but programmes had been laid down. There was thus a fluctuating mass of fluid opinion which might easily crystallise under changed conditions of atmosphere.

At the outset of the Reformation the Papacy scarcely took its religious position seriously; political interests, especially those concerned with Italy, outweighed religious. The short Papacy of Adrian VI was, however, a prophecy of what might happen, and there was a gradual deepening of religious interest at the papal court as the century went on. Into the history of that deepening it is not necessary to enter, but the result was that by the reign of Paul IV the moral tone of the Papacy was raised, and although the Curia was still led by political considerations and still jealous of its political power, there was a real wish to reform abuses. But at the same time in matters of doctrine and worship the Curia moved on the whole away from the mediating party. At the courts of the Empire and of France there was, however, a readiness for some approach to the discontented; the concession of the Chalice to the laity, of clerical marriage, and of the Mass in the vulgar tongue were put forward as making towards peace. Even at the third assembly of the Council of Trent these proposals were in the air, and this fact is only one of many showing a state of opinion less fixed or more sharply divided than we might suppose. The cleavage of opinion was not complete or final until after the Council of Trent, which determined some doctrines in a sense hostile to the Reformation, and also left the authority of the Papacy stronger than before. The Pope had asserted his mastery over the Council; upon points where his power was concerned decision had been avoided, and many difficult matters had been left to him for decision. The help of the new Jesuit body had done great things, and the process by which the Papacy had drawn to itself the powers of the Episcopate was quickened. From the Council of Trent to the Council of the Vatican in 1870 was a step easy to take in logic even if not necessary in doctrine. This was the final answer of the Roman Church to the new age; a reassertion in an enlarged form of that feudal conception the medieval Papacy. The reassertion brought along with it antagonism to the new force of individualism; this was henceforth to be combated and not controlled, to be suppressed rather than utilised.

Another battle which was really fought out at Trent,

although nominally left drawn, was that between the Episcopate and the Papacy. The Spanish bishops especially had wished to put on record the Episcopal claim, and with the help of others from time to time, they had shown some independence. But at Trent a further step was taken along that path by which the Papacy, in great matters of State and in smaller things like canonisation or indulgences, was drawing to itself the powers of the Episcopate with its primitive claims and its national or local sympathies. There was a flicker of the old flame (1763) in the incident of Febronius (which among others the Danish historian Nielsen has so well described) and in the Punctation of Ems; in later days, and even at the Council of the Vatican in 1870, there were murmurs of the same storm, which like other storms has now made its journey across the Atlantic. The two chief stumbling-blocks of the Papacy to-day are the treatment of the national Episcopates under its obedience and of individualism. Now and again there are difficulties such as have arisen sometimes in France, where an Episcopate, less fettered and more independent, might perhaps have been of more service to Church and State. Now and again there have been, above all in the spheres of criticism, of social movements and of politics, cases in which the Papacy has shown the old dread of individualism. The problems of reconciling local liberty and central unity, corporate life and individual freedom, are by no means new. The Papal solution reached in the sixteenth century and put on record at Trent, was the suppression so far as was possible of one element in each case; since then the repetition of the same formula whether by Pope or by Council has possibly made for strength but at the cost of freedom.

Yet the full meaning of these matters is not seen if the Counter-Reformation be viewed simply as a reaction against the Reformation: it was rather a manifestation within the Church of that new life and vigour which had begun to stir in the Middle Ages, and which outside the Church or in opposition to it had resulted in the Protestant movement. After Trent the Roman Church had a higher ideal and greater efficiency (as Bishop Burnet candidly pointed out), and the success of the Counter-Reformation was partly a sign of the inherent strength of the Papacy, partly a sign of the new vigour of religious life. To judge of the movement as a whole we have to take the sixteenth century into one broad view, and it is only when we reach its last quarter that we are conscious of the change in atmosphere, and can feel the power of forces which had begun their work more than a century before. This is the significance of the rise of the Jesuits. Here again we have to trace a growth rather than search for a sudden creation. The creative energy of Loyola was no doubt great, but the inner history and growth of his society reveals perhaps as much the skill of his successor Lainez as it does the conception of the founder; the one, however, is often passed over, while the other is possibly exaggerated. To St. Ignatius the chief thing was the fullest use of his *Spiritual Exercises* : this training moulded the inner man for piety: devotion to the missionary needs of the Papacy came only later when the little band of brothers was shaped into one compact instrument inspired by a single will. But Lainez was more of an orator and a diplomatist, able to reach the reason of men rather than to sway their souls. He was both effective and at home in scenes such as the Colloquy at Poissy or the Council at Trent: from them Loyola would have shrunk and at them he would not have greatly shone. To understand is hard if we limit ourselves too closely to the earlier years of the century. Once more the importance of its later years is borne upon us. There are few histories more fascinating than that of the great society which reconquered so much of the world for the Papacy, and almost conquered the Papacy itself. With wonderful skill it trained and disciplined individuals to be at the disposal of an impersonal system; it seized the benefits and escaped the risks of the new forces which had begun to change the world. In one sense it was an adaptation of what was new, of individualism and of the new educational theories of the Renaissance; in another sense the society itself was formed on the lines of the past and was an outcome of the older world. If we wish, then, to understand the sixteenth century it must even in this case be looked at more as a whole; it must be looked at more as moulded and inspired by the age before it. In the case of England we have come, thanks to many teachers, to see in the reign of Elizabeth the years of settlement, the time when the religious forces have taken their final form, and chosen their true directions. The historical problem is not, of course, solved when those are seen, but its conditions and nature can be known. The Reformation becomes for us a process, and not a crisis: a stage in the gradual growth of man, neither an interruption as some would have it, nor a new creation as others would call it.

This is the historical view of the Reformation for which we must plead. When we take it as a study in origins, as a study in forces and movements, we escape something of the bitterness, even if we lose something of the certainty, which is bound up with parties, and the names of leaders. We cannot, if we take this view, agree with the typically German judgment of the great scholar Harnack—that the history of doctrine ends with Luther. We can judge more calmly what it was he stood for, and we can realise what has been sometimes gained, sometimes lost, since he made himself the symbol of the individual conscience, the symbol of a nation's cause. We think we can see what he saw so clearly, and that we can also see things that he overlooked. To do this makes for calmness, and it makes for growth.

To gain these two great gifts it is not needful to lessen in any way the greatness of the Reformation, to over-estimate or to under-estimate the gains that it made and the risks that it ran. But as we study the forces that shaped it, and see the incidents, sometimes the accidents, above all the never-ceasing influences of politics, that forced or that blocked its path, we must ask ourselves if its sudden outburst or absolute finality is not sometimes asserted too emphatically. It was the outcome of the Middle Ages; it was the beginning of systems under which we live. But there are signs that medieval views of life, formerly shut out too hastily, have a charm for us to-day, and may have a real power for the men of to-morrow. St. Francis has begun to live for us again, when the merchants who elbowed him aside are leaving something more of life to the common man: we understand better the medieval love for the corporate life although we can never forget the Reformation's lesson of individual liberty. In the history of Christianity the obvious has a way of disappearing, assumptions change their dress, and opposites merge themselves in a larger truth. To foretell the future is happily impossible, but to know truly and see fully the past with all its forces and all its life, is to be ready for any future that God in His wisdom may send us. It may be the fortune of that future to place together principles of life, fragments of truth, which the actors in the Reformation thought it impossible to join, which even to us seem far apart. The process of history is the working of God and "His footsteps are not known."

ESSAY II

ERASMUS

SYNOPSIS

ERASMUS

To have been the foremost of scholars when scholarship knew no division of tongues, to have welded together the most spiritual and oldest of studies and the newest critical scholarship of the day, was in itself a great achievement. This is what Erasmus did as he quietly stepped from the medieval into the modern world. Essentially medieval as were the conditions of his life yet he seems essentially modern in the view that he took, and the contrast gives a touch of pathos to his story. In much that has been written about him his medieval background has been left out of sight: in the estimate of his character it is often forgotten how very modern he was. He was so very modern that the Reformation, transacting itself before his eyes, did not close his field of vision: he looked to the foundations of the coming age, to the solid pressure of training that was to form the type of theologian and scholar. This too is often forgotten, and he is, therefore, judged by us, as by his own equals, solely in reference to the Reformation. Thus as a result he is misunderstood: he is pictured as hiding behind his study window, peering into the riot of the market-place below and terrified of the bonfires kindled there. It is not everybody that enjoys a bonfire, and a point of view chosen deliberately and kept with strength is ascribed to mere timidity and indecision.[1]

[1] The letter to Albert of Mainz, of a date probably 1517 and printed as part of preface to the *Ratio Verae Theologiae* (Allen, iii. 175, in part; for a translation see Drummond, ii. 33 f.), is a good illustration of Erasmus's position in face of the Lutheran controversies. He feared to excite new disturbances which often turned out other than intended.

The work of men does not end with their lives: what after-ages think and say of them carries on the tale of what they were and did. Any account of a man should therefore begin with a survey, even if short and summary, of the books written about him. The books written about Erasmus really help us to see him as he was: differing men, too, have seen different sides of his character and his influence: no single writer, whether old or modern, can be taken as a final judge. Furthermore, older writers ought not to be discarded for more modern: their works and their judgments have very often real and essential value. An Essay on Erasmus must begin, then, with a survey and estimate of books, old and new, written about him.

Among the biographies of Erasmus, that by R. B. Drummond (2 volumes, 1873) is the most thorough and valuable, although needing correction on one or two points of later research and in the view of the theology of Erasmus. Of older English lives those by Knight (1726) and Jortin (2 volumes, 1758–62), especially the latter with many quotations in volume ii from Erasmus's works (including the *Julius Exclusus*), are useful. In volume i Jortin summarises the letters under yearly dates. The German and French lives are not more useful than the English, but the French treat the literary side of his life better. H. Durand de Laur, *Érasme, précurseur et initiateur de l'esprit moderne* (2 volumes, Paris, 1872), is a considerable work, the title of which is significant. E. Emerton, *Desiderius Erasmus of Rotterdam* (New York, 1899), is traditional in its views and has a small but careful bibliography. The article on Erasmus in Bayle's Dictionary, written with spirit, is still interesting. There is a useful essay on Erasmus by Milman, who was well able to estimate his work. Froude's *Life and Letters of Erasmus* (1894) is a study by one who appreciated his literary side, but the historical side is open to the same kind of criticism as Froude's other works. The standard edition by Le Clerc (in 10 volumes, Leyden, 1703–6) is superseded for the letters down to June 1519 by Mr. P. S. Allen's most scholarly and model work, *Opus Epistolarum Desi. Erasmi Roterodami*, vols. i–iii (1906, 1910, 1913); the notes and appendices give an immense amount of information not only about Erasmus himself but about his correspondents and the people mentioned. The volumes cover: I. to (July) 1514: II. (June) 1517: III. (June) 1519: IV. (Dec.) 1521: V. (Dec.) 1524: VI. (March) 1527: VII. (Dec.) 1528. It is sad to write these lines soon after the death of our greatest Erasmian scholar, who, in his monument to the learning of Erasmus, has also left us a memorial of himself in this (so unhappily unfinished) edition, one of the finest achievements of English scholarship of all time. We must also gratefully remember the invaluable help given him through many years by Mrs. Allen: she has also edited (1913) the *Praise of Folly*, translated by I. Wilson (1668).

Dr. Allen also edited (Oxford, 1923) *Selections from Erasmus*, to which is prefaced a short but, of course, very accurate life.

His lecture before the British Academy, "Erasmus' Services to Learning" (London, 1925), is invaluable both for its general views and much curious information: it sketches the difficulties of reference for early scholars and their better helps as they passed into the age of printing. It describes the scheme of Erasmus' work as it opened before him and grew upon him: it is specially full on his New Testament and Patristic studies. "His work was always done in heat, under the passion of his demand for knowledge. He read, he wrote 'tumultuarie, praecipitanter.' When he had formed a design, he liked to carry it out 'uno impetu.' " And the mere bulk of his work was amazing, especially as his doctors said he ought to give up work. This lecture should be read along with his "Age of Erasmus" (Oxford, 1914): the lectures given to the Universities of Oxford and London. They are as follows: I. "The Academy of Adwert," near Gröningen, where Wessel (d. 1489),

Agricola, Hegius, Langen, Vrye and others worked. II. "Schools," with many illustrations of the methods of teaching the books and the help provided. III. "Monasteries," specially about Laach, the well-known Benedictine monastery near Andernach, and on the "Monastic Conversations" of Charles Fernand, illustrating the ideals of the day. IV. "Universities": this is mainly on the career of Erasmus himself: incidentally we read of the presence of a Greek scribe in England about 1470, discovered by Dr. M. R. James (p. 121): there was also another here some twenty years later. V. "Erasmus's Life and Work." This is most important for the growth around him of his work, especially of his New Testament studies. As he said himself towards the end of his *Enchiridion Militis Christiani*: "It was not for mere fame that in my youth I reached out after the polite literature of the Ancients, and, not without many vigils, gained a little mastery of Greek and Latin. It has long been my dearest wish to cleanse the Temple of the Lord of barbarous ignorance and to my utmost power beautify it with exotic treasures by which noble minds may be fired with a love of the divine Scriptures." It is interesting to note that comparing the styles of Jerome and Cicero he seemed to feel something lacking in the prince of eloquence himself. Many details about which we here learn so much must be passed over. But at Basle, which Beatus Rhenanus called " βασίλεια, the queen of cities," he made important friendships, the Amorbachs and Froben, great printers with whom he made his home: the father, John Amorbach, died on Christmas Day, 1513, but his sons were growing up to take his place.

VI. "Force and Fraud." This lecture sketches the violence of the age and specially of the mercenary bands. These undisciplined and yet too well-disciplined troops burnt and ravaged widely. The mentality of the Middle Ages is typified by an example given us by another great scholar, Denifle. A Brandenburg Prince said to have burnt more towns and villages than any other leader of mercenaries justified the use of fire in warfare as completing the task. Fire was to warfare, he said, what the Magnificat was to Evensong, that is to say, its very centre and essence. So devotion could exist together with cruelty. Fraud and insincerity in private life is exemplified by literary instances, and here Dr. Allen discusses the explicit ascription by Erasmus of a letter from Ammonius, an able scholar, to Lord Mountjoy, their common patron, who seems to have written English with difficulty enough and who was therefore not likely to write Latin. This ascription of Latin scholarship to the peer might seem to discount the same praise given by Erasmus to Henry VIII. It is well known that he was accused of having written for the King the answer to Luther, written after the *De Captivitate Babylonica* had appeared. But Erasmus said that Henry was scholar enough to have written it himself. Most opinions have accepted Erasmus as clear of complicity, but Dr. Allen, whose opinion must have great weight, gives a verdict of "not proven." For myself I am not quite ready to accept this. Oddly enough Erasmus was also accused of having written Luther's works on the other side, but leaving Latinity aside the violence of their tone compels a verdict of "not guilty" in this case.

Lecture VII deals with Private Life and Manners: and IX with Pilgrimages. The uncertainty of life, due largely to wars, famines and pestilences, cast its shadow over all. Among its results was the frequency and repetition of marriages (which incidentally makes the record of Henry VIII seem less peculiar), and this is illustrated from a wide field with Dr. Allen's great knowledge of medieval letters. With Pilgrimages we are on more familiar ground, but here too we are told much that is fresh. Lecture VIII—the Point of View—illustrates from the case of Erasmus the indifference of a traveller to the beautiful scenes of Nature or of Art by which he passed. But he, like Paul and some other early

travellers, was more intent upon men and Humanity at
large than upon aught else. Possibly this may be the
explanation of what seems puzzling or even unnatural.
Lecture XI sketches the intercourse between Erasmus and
Bohemians, beginning with an invitation to Prague from a
Bohemian gentleman, Slechta: an account was given from
an orthodox standpoint of the Bohemian Brethren and their
teaching. His proffered host was hostile to them, but
Erasmus, who spoke with charity, was also anxious not to
appear too friendly. With their dislike of abuses in the
Church he sympathised, but it was not for him, he said, to
arbitrate between the Church and critics who had severed
themselves from it.

Lecture X on the Transalpine Renaissance is the most
important even where all are essential. Dr. Allen thinks that
the Renaissance has suffered from a reaction due to the very
proper attempt by critics and historians to do justice to the
Middle Ages. Hence some historians, he thought, seemed to
minimise the effects and grandeur of the Renaissance. He
himself had noted how, with the Renaissance, "the stream
of personal record," hidden underground for centuries, had
emerged, giving us history from the individual standpoint,
not from charters and records of institutions. This is a
sound and fundamental doctrine too often forgotten.

But Dr. Allen is concerned here with the difference of
Transalpine from the Italian Renaissance, and he gives an
excellent, if all too summary, sketch of a long chapter in the
history of thought, beginning, we may say, where Sir
Samuel Dill left off. The real Classical Age had been
followed by that of Rhetoric, with its efflorescence, specially
in Gaul. When the Renaissance came, the great Classics
were studied afresh. The Italian side of the Revival has been
well portrayed by Dr. Jacob Burckhardt in his *Civilisation
of the Renaissance in Italy*, now in an English dress: it had
its good and its bad side. On the good side the great redis-
covery of the Classics meant something to Italians that it

46

could not mean to Transalpine races. For Italians the heritage of Rome, of the Imperial City, of Imperial supremacy was theirs alone. In it the newer races had no share. So the Italians looked down on the others, and if these turned naturally and well to study their own early history, as they did with benefit and pride, the compensation had only a lesser glory. Transalpine scholars and students read the Classics for what they could learn, but with a proud sense of kinship: Italians read them with a sense of ownership and pride. Moreover, Scholasticism had been a creation of the North. Italy had been the foster-mother, at any rate, of the Canon Law and other lands had joined its train. But most of the great names of Scholasticism, on the other hand, belong to the Northern races.

The Church had never felt quite happy in opening the Pagan Classics to its youthful scholars, and the interest of the Scholastics was rather in matter, thought and argument than in elegance and form, but the latter were dearer to the Humanists. Their extreme wing, the Ciceronians, who would have everything said precisely as Cicero had said it, exposed themselves to ridicule as Erasmus proved in his *Ciseronianus* (1528). But, on the other hand, the Scholastics had formed a technical language of their own, passing, at its worst, into the barbarous jargon of those badly educated monks who hated the "poets." Such linguists were easy game for the Humanists like Ulric von Hutten (who had no strong dislike for Paganism) and Crotus Rubianus in the *Epistolae Obscurorum Virorum*. The scholars, therefore, who went to Italy and came home to the North carrying the new enthusiasm had strenuous opposition to encounter. The Schoolmen considered them impertinent, the Church counted them immoral. And the struggle went on well into the sixteenth century. Gabriel Biel, of Tübingen, "the last of the Schoolmen" as he was called although many lesser men followed him, died in 1495, and Luther, among other young students, was brought up on his doctrine. The invention of printing (*c.* 1455) is the border-line between the two Renaissances: the Italian had run half its course, the German had scarcely begun.

But the invention of printing made at once a change which was slowly realised and gradually grew in force. When different scholars might be using different and possibly erroneous texts, accuracy was difficult and confusion probable. A new reign, one of accuracy and uniformity, set in. Erasmus was fortunate in coming at the beginning of this new age with its new power.

It may seem that I have given too great a space to these lectures. But the greatest of Erasmian scholars had a right to speak with authority, for no one could so well enter into the mind of Erasmus as he with his continued labour of loving industry. He was able to see for himself and to show to us exactly how, and exactly where his age had influenced him, and so we come gratefully and easily for ourselves to understand better both the man and his age. The learning and the sweep of this book give us the distilled essence, as it were, of the seven large invaluable volumes of the *Epistolae*. We might call them the "verbal Illustrations" to his great work. There is a later life: *Erasmus, a Study of his Life, Ideals and Place in History*, by Professor Preserved Smith (Cornell University: New York and London, 1923), with a good Bibliography. It is particularly useful for its full treatment of the relations between Erasmus and Luther. Neither the Lutherans nor their opponents could understand the neutrality which Erasmus professed and kept. All this the author is peculiarly able to treat of, as it was after some years' study of the Reformation and especially of Luther that he returned to his earlier Erasmian studies. Hence he is able to estimate rightly the place of Erasmus in history. This is the great merit of the book. But, a little like the earlier biographer Drummond, he seems to my mind to over-stress an opposition between Christian dogma which really inspires a moral life, and practical morality itself. I

48

should doubt whether to the mind of Erasmus the two could exist either at all or for long in isolation.

The literary history of the *Colloquies* is best given in chap. xi of this book (p. 286 *seq.*). The first of them was written in 1497. And Beatus Rhenanus published them at Basle (1518). Later editions, both from the Froben press, followed in 1519 and 1522, and later editions were enlarged. The English translation by N. Bailey (1733) was conveniently reprinted in 1877. Intended to help learners of Latin, the work shows Erasmus turning to the use of dialogue as in the *Antibarbari*.

Mr. Nichols's *Epistles of Erasmus*, a translation into English of the letters down to December 1518 (3 volumes, 1918), is sound and learned. Seebohm's *Oxford Reformers* (3rd ed., 1887), dealing with the fellow work of Colet, Erasmus, and More, broke up a new field, and summarises the theological work of Erasmus: the main points of criticism are spoken of in this article. There is a chapter (vol. i, ch. x) in Brewer's *Reign of Henry VIII* (2 volumes, 1884), a chapter (iii) in Lord Acton's *Lectures on Modern History*, and an article by Dean Hutton in the *Quarterly Review* (October 1905). The *Cambridge Modern History* (vol. i, *The Renaissance*) has a chapter (xvii) by Dr. M. R. James which brings in Erasmus. Imbart de la Tour's *Les Origines de la Réforme*, vol. ii, has much about Erasmus. A bibliography of Erasmus's own writings is given in the *Oxford Reformers* and of the subject generally in Allen's *Opus Epistolarum Des. Erasmi* (already mentioned). A. Richter's *Erasmus-Studien* (Dresden, 1891) and Nolhac, *Érasme en Italie* (2nd ed., Paris, 1898), are most useful, although all their discussions are utilised by Allen and by Nichols.

Desiderius Erasmus Roterodamus: Ausgewählte Werke: von Hajo Holborn und Annemarie Holborn (Munich, 1933), is published under the Commission for the study of the Reformation and Counter-Reformation. It contains the *Enchiridion Militis Christiani:* the Prefaces to the New

Testament (*Paraclesis, Methodus* and *Apologia*): the *Ratio seu Methodus Compendio perveniendi ad* Veram *Theologiam*. The editing may be depended upon and the volume of some 320 pages is convenient in size.

A pamphlet of only 24 pages by Dr. Rudolf Pfeiffer: *Humanitas Erasmiana* (Leipzig, 1931), is useful and instructive far beyond its size. The author had studied the Humanism of Erasmus at the Bibliothek Warburg in 1926 and later (1928–9) carried it on at Baden and in Bavaria. He had started naturally with the early work, the *Antibarbari*, written in Erasmus's monastic period. His youthful draft was altered and turned into a dialogue, meant to be in four books, two of which were written at Bologna. But manuscripts left with Richard Pace in Italy were lost, and so Book I was published separately.[1] By 1523 he had recovered the beginning of Book II from England and the end of it from Bruges. But he never regained the whole, although Ascham wrote to Froben in 1551 saying that he had seen a more complete MS at Cambridge the year before.

But Dr. Pfeiffer traces with fine scholarship the conception of *Humanitas* which was the ideal of Erasmus. The scholar's work demanded peace and quiet: sound learning was from first to last his ideal: it was to be the foundation for future ages. It was disturbed by the ignorant opposition to the "poets" as humanists were called, and it was disturbed later still more by the opposition to the New Testament work of Erasmus, and by the violent disturbance due to Lutheran controversy. But, to my mind, it is significant to see the humanism of Erasmus taking, as he grew older, a more theological direction, although his standpoint remained always the same. If Scholarship was to do its work for the world it must understand mankind (Humanity): there must be a wide and tolerant charity with no narrowness of particularism. It was a splendid vision. It demanded peace between men and an

[1] For the history of the work, see Allen, vol. i, Ep. 30 and iv, Ep. 1110 (the preface to all that was published (Book I)).

eager readiness to see the good in all. For Theologians this was a sacred duty, and so the early dream gradually grew but the elements of the work around him changed. A man might be a finished Greek or Latin scholar and yet miss the most essential thing of all, and that was sacred letters and Theology. This was the sacred ideal.

Dr. Wallace K. Ferguson (Assistant-Professor of History in the University of New York) has given us a useful selection in his *Erasmi Opuscula* (The Hague, 1933), intended as a supplement to the *Opera Omnia*: it gives us (*a*) some of the early poems; (*b*) the *Julius Exclusus* and an Epigram on Pope Julius II; (*c*) the *Hieronymi Stridonensis Vita*, which has value from the place St. Jerome held in his heart of Erasmus; (*d*) the *Dialogus Bilinguium ac trilinguium* (which fits in well with Dr. R. Pfeiffer's *Humanitas Erasmiana*); (*e*) What will attract most readers are two works on the Lutheran controversy: the *Acta Academiae Louvaniensis contra Lutherum* and the *Axiomata Erasmi pro Causa Martini Lutheri*. These show us Erasmus striving to keep his neutral and pacific standpoint even when attacked by both sides. His plan of pacification was a council, and this reminds us of his oddly unfinished letter to Adrian VI. Adequate discussions are given in the Introductions and many references to recent works. These are specially useful on the Lutheran section and form an excellent guide to the literature on the subject.

In the *English Historical Review* (vol. x, 1895) there is an admirable article on Erasmus in Italy by the Rev. E. H. R. Tatham, the biographer of Petrarch.

Yet there is no man better able to speak for himself: letters which had a marketable value in their own day have an even greater value for us: the *Colloquies* and the *Praise of Folly* have not yet lost their original freshness and charm. It is best to let him speak for himself, and it is pleasant to think that English scholarship in the edition of the epistles by Mr. P. S. Allen and in the English translations by the late Mr. Nichols has made it easier for us to listen to him aright.

Born at Rotterdam, 27 October 1466 or 1467, in the house of his grandmother, with an unmarried mother, with a father who afterwards became a monk on hearing a false rumour of the mother's death, he inherited membership in a divided family on one side, and on the other his father's gaiety of disposition and love of manuscripts. His first school, entered at four years of age, was Gouda, but that was left for the post of choir-boy at Utrecht. At nine years he went to a more celebrated school at Deventer, where was the earliest foundation of the Brethren of the Common Life:[1] Erasmus's school was one attached to a church and some of his teachers belonged to the brethren. This society had an influence, not only upon Erasmus, but upon many others, that deserves especial stress. We very often assume too great a break in passing from medieval education and medieval thought to those of the Reformation age. But after all one age changes very slowly into another, and it is the business of the student to search for continuity and not save himself trouble by postulating revolution or sudden creations. Among the many less perceptible means by which the medieval world moulded the modern was this Brotherhood of the Common Life. Its work was quiet and directed

[1] In this Essay I had used the term Brethren of the Common Lot, following Ullmann: *Reformers before the Reformation* (T. and T. Clark, 1855), ii. 70, in his Life of Gerhard Groot; and A. W. Haddan, *Remains* (Oxford, 1876), p. 412. The term "Common Life" then seemed open to misunderstanding, as English readers might take it in the monastic sense, implying rules for a thoroughly common life; but to monks the Brethren were opposed and, although they had a common aim in a life more or less ordered, they had not a common life in the fuller monastic sense. I think that now, however, the misunderstanding is less likely, and I have, therefore, used the more usual form. The Brethren had a common fund; they were called Collationarie because of the addresses given to their pupils (see Nichols, i. 18. For the letters of Groot, see J. Mulder, *Epistolae Gerardi Magni* (Utrecht, 1930)).

to form individuals, not to gain great results at once: it was continuous, its members were not, so to speak, always altering their triposes, transforming their schools, or changing their ideals of education; their work was thorough and it was effective. The connection of Erasmus with the brotherhood was more than a chronological fact.[1]

The brotherhood was founded by Gerhard Groot[2] at Deventer about 1380; it was inspired by the true spirit of mysticism (a feeling which found its best home in the Middle Ages) and by the idea of brotherhood which had wrought so many revivals in the same Burgundian lands. From the days of Gerhard onwards love of the Scriptures and of the Fathers —shown by the constant copying of manuscripts—was a special feature of its work. Another was the education of the young. Not only at Deventer but also at 's Hertogenbosch (Bois-le-Duc), where Erasmus was afterwards for two years, and at Steyn near Gouda, had they some of their celebrated schools. So great was their success that in some places even the girls sang Latin songs in the streets. Nor were their methods dry: the classics themselves were placed in the hands of their pupils, and this was specially done by Alexander Hegius at Deventer. Latin they had conquered and towards Greek they advanced. In the Netherlands and not in Italy is to be sought the true birthplace of the German Renaissance, which was not artistic, was certainly not pagan, but was from first to last practical and educational in its aims, keeping throughout in close touch with theology. If on the side of mysticism it brought forth Thomas à Kempis[3]

[1] An interesting analogy for the influence of medieval education upon Reformation, and even more modern, scholarship is given by the researches of the late Mr. A. F. Leach; see his *Schools of Medieval England* (1915) and his other publications. Many schools, supposed to be modern, were really medieval foundations, in some cases with a long history.

[2] For the letters of Gerhard Groot, see *Epistolae Gerardi Magni* by J. Mulder (Utrecht 1930). Ullmann's *Reformers before the Reformation* (T. and T. Clark, Edinburgh), ii. 79, has a good life.

[3] The evidence goes to show that Thomas à Kempis (of Kempen)

on the side of learning it brought forth Rudolph
Agricola.

From 1476 to 1482, six of the most susceptible years of
life, from the age of nine to fifteen, first at Deventer, with its
traditions and its occasional visits from Zinthius and Rudolph
Agricola,[1] and afterwards at Bois-le-Duc, with its memories
of days when it could count 2,000 scholars, Erasmus was
under the power of this system.[2] A simple living piety, a
mysticism which never lost hold upon practical life, inspired
it, and its motto was that " liberty of spirit was the greatest
good in the spiritual life." About minute points the founder
cared not to speculate, and on many secondary matters (I
will only instance confession and pilgrimages) the tone of
thought was independent. Things were judged more by
their practical value than by the weight of custom that lay
behind them. It is curious that the brothers were often
called after St. Jerome—the Father for whom Erasmus had
formed a special liking at an early stage;[3]—and this Father,
upon whose biblical labours and theological position

---

was the copyist, not the author, of the complete *Imitatio*. The history
of the manuscript points (1) to its being a composite work (which is
also to be seen from internal evidence) and (2) to its original home being
Italy. The background of the discussion is the medieval view of
plagiarism; writers used preceding works freely without any prejudice
against doing so and without any idea of a writer's moral copyright.
This was the case with writers of chronicles and also with theologians.
What Thomas says of himself need only mean that he compiled or
copied the work with the idea of rendering it useful.

[1] See Allen, i. 581.

[2] For the dates of Erasmus's school life, see Allen, i. 584; Nichols, i.
16 f.

[3] There is a useful note on Erasmus and St. Jerome in Allen, ii. 210,
as complete as most of this writer's admirable work is. As early as June
1489 (see Ep. 22, Allen, i. 103) Erasmus says he had read St. Jerome's
letters and copied them out; and this field of study was never neglected
onwards down to 1512. The correspondence with Cornelius Gerard is
most important: see Allen, i. 586–7; Nichols, i. 75. For Erasmus's
imitation of Jerome, Nichols, i. 87. He preferred Jerome's style to
Cicero's, much as Valla did Quintilian. So did Croke and Linacre.
See Bass Mullinger, *Cambridge*, i. 529 and note.

Erasmus endeavoured to form himself, was their patron saint. And it should not be forgotten that the brotherhood had been attacked (at the Council of Constance, for instance) by the monastic orders, and also by the Dominicans, for belonging to no special Order. An attempted rule, that of the Canons of the Common Life, had shown little stability, and the brethren—Tertiaries, so to speak—were only semi-monastic at most. If the monks criticised them, they in their turn had a keen eye for the failings of the Regulars, and here again their influence upon Erasmus was greater, perhaps, than he supposed.

It is true that the express opinion of Erasmus in his letter to Grunnius[1] disparages their schools, representing them as mere traps for monasteries. The letter was, however, written with a special bias and was meant to influence Leo X towards releasing him from the troublesome obligation to wear his "habit" or for some even greater privilege. Quite apart from this, it is very difficult to give a completely fair account of one's own development and to assign a proper weight to the influences which have formed one's character; it is not everyone who can write an *Apologia pro vita sua* or describe himself in the past. Moreover, Erasmus himself tells us that at Deventer he got the first taste of a better training,[2] and he arrived at Bois-le-Duc, a more backward school than Deventer, "knowing more than his teachers." A boy of thirteen does not usually know by heart, as he did,[3] all the works of Terence and Horace. Adrian VI was a product of

[1] See Ep. 447, Allen, ii. 291–3 n.; Nichols, i. 20 f. and ii, ch. xxx. Erasmus wished to hold benefices and therefore he needed dispensation on account of his birth, but he wished to say little of this. He had a dispensation from his "habit," but this may have applied only to Italy. He may have outstepped its provisions, but probably he wished to be safeguarded against an enforced return to Steyn.

[2] In his earlier letters there is no expression of discontent with his early schools. See Nichols, i. 88. This is curiously parallel to Luther and his early monastic life.

[3] So we are told by Beatus Rhenanus in a letter to Hermann, bishop of Cologne (see Nichols, i. 36, 37).

the same school of Deventer, and a system which gained the praise of Gerson at an earlier date, of Luther and Melanchthon at a later, cannot have been wholly bad in the days of Erasmus. For its very method aimed at forming scholars such as Erasmus was, and if an Erasmus was produced it was surely not by accident. Left without father and mother, urged to the step by guardians who cared more for his property than for himself, in 1486 he made his profession as a Regular in the Augustinian monastery of Steyn; and although the society was uncongenial and its manners rough, he carried on the study of good letters with his friend William Herman as a comrade. A question is suggested by Dr. Allen[1] which cannot be passed over. Some of the earlier letters, especially those to Servatius, raise a doubt as to whether Erasmus had passed morally unharmed through his early days at Steyn, where Servatius had been a much-loved comrade. Some later allusions to his later time in Paris might also be taken as implying a past not stainless. The friendly affection was warmer on the side of Erasmus, and Servatius as a correspondent grew gradually cooler: towards the end Erasmus for his part mostly sends exhortations to study. Must we then rank him with Aeneas Sylvius (Pius II), who had a past, as Gregory of Heimburg reminded him, unfitted for a Pope, or with Theodore Beza, who in youth had written so licentiously as to shame a theologian? For my part I should judge Erasmus more favourably than Dr. Allen seems inclined to. Youthful friendships in collegiate days are often strong, and might be more so in the case of one who, like Erasmus, had no pleasant family life or home friends. Moreover, later scandal only charged him with a love of wine, and for that there is no foundation. Had there been anything against him on the side of morality, his later foes were bitter enough to bring it up and we should have had more to discuss. Sound divinity, into which he threw himself more and more as years went by, may well have had,

[1] In vol. iii, *Appendix I* (Letters to Servatius, Francis and Sasbond).

as it should, great moral value even in the society of young men as licentious as many of his circle must have been. At the age of eighteen he condensed a work of Valla's on the teaching of Latin,[1] and even thus early he had gained his great taste for St. Jerome. But his study of Valla was not solely philological. He says he was exploring in an old monastic library, when "(for no coverts afford more delightful sport) some game of no common sort fell into my net." It was Valla's notes on the New Testament, and these were a great delight to him.[2]

But the Netherlands with their shifting politics were then, as later, merely a stepping-stone to other lands, and in 1491 Erasmus entered the service of the bishop of Cambrai,[3] a patron who is described as lacking in generosity and who after all did not open to his client the expected road to Italy. In 1492 Erasmus was ordained priest, and between this date and 1496 he went to the university of Paris, which had still much of its old reputation, and where Greek was taught as it had been since 1458, even if now inefficiently under Hermonymus, "twofold times a Greek, always hungry and asking heavy fees."[4] His experiences there, described later in letters and in the *Colloquies*, at the college of Montaigu, and at a hostel for poor students, are well known.[5] The hard life left its mark in illness, and the profitable care of private pupils, among whom Thomas Grey[6] and William Blunt,

---

[1] For his study of Valla, see Nichols, i. 69; for the epitome, pp. 86–7; Allen, i. 587.

[2] See Nichols, i. 381; Allen, i. 407.

[3] Allen, i, app. v, p. 587.

[4] In Epistle to Antony, abbot of St. Bertin (Nichols, i. 314; Allen, i. 353). On Erasmus at Paris see Nichols, i, cc. iv, v, and vi.

[5] See the *Colloquies* under Ἰχθυοφαγία : *George*; "Out of what hencoop or cave do you come?" *Lewis*. "Why do you ask me such a question?" *George*. "Because you have been so poorly fed: you are so thin, a person may see through you and you crackle with dryness. Whence come you?" *Lewis*. "I come from the College of Montaigu."

[6] Not, as often said to have been, a member (at any rate a legitimate one) of the Dorset family. See Nichols, i. 115; Allen, i. 174 (Ep. 58).

Lord Mountjoy, were the richest, was, after all, a distraction from the main end of his life. Some offers he refused; no bribe shall lead him away from sacred studies: "he had not gone to the university to teach or to make money, but to learn,"[1] and to learn, with the far-off hope of a journey to Italy before him,[2] he was resolved.

It should be noted, I think, that Erasmus was essentially cosmopolitan because he was essentially medieval: the traditions of the Empire lingered longest about the scholastic world, and Erasmus, with no fatherland to speak of or rather with a fatherland that had once been German,[3] and had scarcely yet grown to be Dutch, fell easily into the scholar's place in such a world and such a brotherhood of learning. If he missed the inspiration of patriotism, he was equally removed from the isolation that sometimes goes with it, and so Erasmus, who thought in the same Latin which he spoke,[4] is the finished type of a medieval scholar, a type which gradually died out after the Reformation and the separation of the nations, although here and there it left a stray representative, and a stray representative only, in such scholars as Casaubon.

To this stage of his career belong especially the most painful letters of his life, those which deal with his patrons and his relations to them: the stingy Englishman from whom much was expected and little gained, the Lady of Veere, the owner of Tournehem, and the abbot of St. Bertin. He would prefer, he tells Batt, "a certain amount of cash sent with 'his letter' to a most ample sum on paper."[5] There were few, he

[1] See Epistle to Nicholas Werner (Allen, i. 159; Nichols, i. 118).

[2] See Epistle to Arnold Bostius (Allen, i. 202; Nichols, i. 160).

[3] For Erasmus's scanty German, see Ep. 635, Allen, i. 215, Le Clerc; for his linguistic knowledge, Richter, *Erasmus-Studien*, app. B, p. xix f.

[4] So did Isaac Williams at a later day. In writing an English essay he thought it out in Latin and then translated it into English (see his *Autobiography*). England and its old schools had a little kept up the traditions of the seventeenth century, which in its turn had not broken touch with the Middle Ages. The disuse of the study of later Latin was the cause of much division in thought and taste. [5] Nichols, i. 180.

says, who would give enough to maintain a man able to write books worthy of immortality. "Tell my Lady," he writes to Batt, "that I cannot for shame expose my state to her," and then he describes himself as he really was.[1] The constant gifts of money from great people, always sought for but not always gained; the caution of such as Archbishop Warham (afterwards a generous friend), who suspected that a book offered to him for dedication had been previously given elsewhere—these are the unpleasant features of the medieval method of endowing research and supporting literature. All we can say, I think, is that Erasmus came through the process with less loss of dignity than many others, and kept his independence better than most. If towards the end of his life we read less of this alms-seeking and alms-giving, it is due not only to his having gained a surer footing, but also to the growth of the printing-press. Aldus at Venice and then Froben at Basle took the place of patrons: the printing-press, it is true, did much to destroy the copyist-scholar of the Common Life, but the printer's home at Basle with its large collection of manuscripts and with its congenial group of scholars assured to Erasmus some independence and freedom from the wearier cares of life. In a wider and a sounder view of the possibilities of literature and a new way of gaining means to live, we see the chief trace of his Italian career. He came into touch with printers, who were then publishers and also supporters of writers, and what he had learnt from Aldus at Venice he afterwards could apply to Froben at Basle.

In 1499–1500 Erasmus paid his first visit to England on the invitation of Thomas Grocyn. Here he found a "thick crop of ancient learning";[2] and in another direction he soon became a tolerable huntsman and no bad rider, even if we

[1] See the whole letter in Nichols, i. 298 f.; Allen, i. 325. He wants help to get his doctor's degree in Italy, but especially for "the restoration of the works of St. Jerome and the revival of true theology."

[2] See Epp. 456, 457, and 540 in Allen, vol. ii. Bishop Fisher admired Reuchlin. See also Nichols, iii. 149.

find him on a later visit leaving the care of his horse to others and especially to his friend William Gunnell at Landbeach, where Parker was afterwards Rector: it may be noticed that he had also sometimes cause to regret his dealings with those who knew more of horses than he did himself. How the English ladies kissed him on introduction and he shamelessly told is a well-known story. There were other sufferings too: our houses were not warm enough, and the discomforts of a country house at Landbeach, whither he long afterwards withdrew from Cambridge through fear of plague, soon drove him thence back to town. From our customs officers he also suffered: after his first visit he was allowed to return with only a limited amount of gold, the rest being confiscated in the interests of "the King's treasure." He was therefore obliged to publish quickly a small work which he had in hand, and this was afterwards enlarged into the *Adages*. On a later return journey his portmanteau containing his manuscript of St. Jerome was bundled into another boat and caused him many misgivings. As we read and feel with him we seem to be in almost modern times.

It was on this first visit that he made friends with Colet and More; thus forming the brotherhood which Seebohm described so well. But there is one criticism of Seebohm's book which must be made. He depicts Colet as the moving spirit of the little band, so far as they had a common aim at all. Yet long before Erasmus saw Colet he had marked out, indeed his teachers had marked out for him, the path of biblical study and of a living theology. Even his dislike of the scholastic method, the scientific jargon, the technical terminology of the Middle Ages, had existed before, and it should be remembered that the Common Life stood far removed from scholastic lines. Writing to his friend and pupil, Thomas Grey, before his visit to England, he said:[1] "I, the famous theologian, have become a Scotist . . . you

---

[1] Nichols, i. 141 f., Allen, i. 190. This letter is a good description of Erasmus's views, and the early date, August 1497, may be noted.

have not the least notion of a theological slumber. . . ."
And he says of Epimenides, "he also published theological
books, and in them tied such syllogistic knots that he could
never untie himself." Epimenides slept, it is true, but "most
of the theologians of to-day never waken at all." Epimenides has come to life again in Scotus. Erasmus himself is
striving to become a theologian of their type: "I am doing
my utmost not to say anything in pure Latin, to give up all
grace and wit, and I think I am succeeding. There is hope
they will at last own Erasmus." But he kept his wit, while
some of them had never much to lose. All this language of
his is, he explains, only a jest at the expense of the scholastic
theologians of the day, with their brains rotten, their speech
barbarous, their minds dull, their learning thorny, their
manners rude, their life savouring of hypocrisy, and their
hearts as black as night. Erasmus and Colet were brothers
indeed: like true friends they thought the same and wished
the same, but Erasmus in his ideal of theology owed little or
no original inspiration to the great Englishman. The tribute
Erasmus laid upon the grave of his lamented friend was great
indeed, but it is matched by another which he paid to the
memory of another, of Vitrarius,[1] the Franciscan of St.
Omer, from whom he had derived an impulse towards a
study of St. Paul and also of the Fathers, and whose re-
semblance to Colet was strong: he was a monk out of
harmony with the level tones around him, the very ideal of
the truest monk.

Among the names of his earliest friends and constant
correspondents appear three: Cornelius Gerard, Cornelius
Aurelius, and Cornelius Lopsen.[2] The insight of Mr. Allen
has succeeded in identifying all these as the same friend
under different names, for "Aurelius" was the equivalent of
"van Gouda," although he had previously been held to be
distinct from the two others. Cornelius had urged Erasmus

---

[1] See Drummond, i. 123 f.; Allen, i. 372 (note to Ep. 163, l. 3), and
Ep. 169.   [2] See Allen, i. 92, and app. iv; also Nichols, i. 56–8.

to read the Fathers, and above all the Epistles of St. Jerome. In reply Erasmus says he has read and even copied them out carefully, and this is one indication among many of his early bent towards such studies.[1] In the Epistle to Grunnius we have the pathetic story of Erasmus and his youthful friend sitting up late in their little cells by dim candle-light and studying together classics and the works of their beloved Fathers.

The next years 1500–3 are spent at Paris and in short visits which had little permanent effect upon his life. In 1503–4 he is for the first time at Louvain, where he had many friends, Dorpius and others, and where the University afterwards became the stronghold of conservatism. In 1506 he was once more in England and on this visit added Tunstall and Warham to his friends and patrons, while he also paid a short visit to Cambridge. England he left for Italy in charge of the son of the King's doctor, Boerio. It was naturally the Renaissance side of Roman life which most impressed him, and we may consider that his reputation was now nearing the height at which it stood so long. To visit Italy was the dream of every scholar, especially of those who, as Beatus Rhenanus assures us Erasmus was, were mainly self-taught.[2] And Erasmus himself tells us that his mind was in Italy, which he visited chiefly to improve his Greek. But Italian wars, the prevalent plague, and varied misfortunes spoilt his visit; moreover, the charge of the pupils, although they had a staff of servants, was a hindrance to his freedom. From the common life of the country he stood apart; Italian he spoke even less than German:[3] of both languages

[1] See Allen, i. 103, and Nichols, i. 75.

[2] Beatus Rhenanus says in his life of Erasmus that save for the rudiments, he had been self-taught. For Beatus see Allen, *Age of Erasmus*, 154 f. For the Italian visit I am indebted chiefly to Nolhac's admirable book, *Érasme en Italie*, and to the notes in Allen's *Epistolae Erasmi*. See also Tathurn's article in *E.H.R.* At Bologna, in the house of Paolo Bombasio, Erasmus studied Greek for himself with the help of his friends. On Bombasio see Nichols, i. 427, and Drummond, i. 169.

[4] He says, "Italice non intelligo" (in 1535). He could not write

he knew a few words, just enough for the ordinary purposes of travel, but, for instance when he met the Elector of Saxony, Spalatin had to interpret for him. And at Rome it was the company of the learned, especially of Tommaso Inghirami, a librarian of the Vatican, in which he most delighted.[1] Significantly enough, he writes to Aldus Manutius expressing surprise that he had not so far published the New Testament.[2] It is clear that while Italy, and the Aldine Press as suiting Italian taste, were chiefly interested in secular literature, Erasmus was already turning chiefly to sound theology and sacred learning. But Rome he rightly held, as his correspondents did, to be the common fatherland of learned men.[3] But save for the friends[4] he made and his visit to the Aldine Press, Italy had been a disappointment. At Rome he might have stayed for good, and later there was talk of a bishopric in Sicily, but the lines of his life would have had to be greatly altered in such a case. At Venice he visited the press of Aldus, and (as I am told is sometimes done even now) he pretended there to be only an agent for Erasmus without full power to treat for him. The generosity of the publisher-printer, however, did away with the need for any such subterfuge; he stayed there some time and the third edition of his *Adages* appeared as the result (1508). At Venice also he came to know Aleander, a much-admired cosmopolitan scholar, whom he at first highly esteemed and

---

easily in his native tongue: so he says in a letter to Lang; see Nichols, i. 153, and Allen, i. 216. He only wrote in bad French and disliked the pronunciation: see Nichols, i. 236, and Allen, i. 287.

[1] Erasmus speaks of the libraries at Rome in a letter to Cardinal Lorenzo Campeggio in 1520. Elsewhere there was a great dearth of sacred books and in Italy few were being printed (Allen: *Ep.* 1167, iv. 400).

[2] Nolhac, p. 98; Allen, i. 438.

[3] Riario to Erasmus: "Roma communis literatorum omnium et patria est et altrix et euectrix" (1515): Allen, ii. 118.

[4] John Watson, writing to Erasmus in 1516, says he found Erasmus celebrated in Italy, and that people were proud to have met him. See Nicholls, ii. 334; Allen, ii. 314 f.

recommended but whom at a later date he thought to be the centre of a conspiracy against him.

In England he had made more "learned, obliging, virtuous and sincere friends than in the whole of the world." In Italy he had to meet a new world: Bologna, where he stayed a year and saw the triumphal entry of Julius II in 1506 (Nov. 11), he disliked, but his friendship with the Greek scholar Bombasio ("a golden-hearted man, the truest friend") was some compensation. He was now passing definitely from his classical period to his theological work. But he corresponded with Aldus about a revised edition of his later translations of the *Hecuba* and *Iphigenia in Aulis* of Euripides which had been very badly printed at Paris, and later at Venice (Sept. 1, 1508) he printed his *Adagiorum Chiliades* or *Adages*, a work which gradually grew. And its growth was bound up with his steady mastery of Greek. The literature of proverbs is ancient and extensive:[1] the wisdom of Solomon did not stand alone in the East, and the unspoken literature is greater than the printed. Isaac Disraeli gave them a long section in his interesting *Curiosities of Literature*, and Archbishop Trench treated them in a well-appreciated book. Erasmus in his successive enlargements from some eight hundred to over three thousand proverbs added much of his own views in all kinds of subjects, talking as it were to his growing public, so that we learn as much of his own thought as of that of centuries past. And besides this it was a useful introduction first to Latin and then to Greek at a time when inquiring students had little to help them. No work of his sold better, comparatively expensive as it was, and fresh editions were repeatedly called for.

From Venice he went to Padua to be tutor to Alexander Stewart, an illegitimate son of James IV of Scotland, and

[1] I. Disraeli, *Curiosities of Literature*, iii. 32–65. Archbishop Trench wrote *The Lessons of Proverbs* (1853), which went into seven editions. For Erasmus's knowledge of Greek, Allen i. 592. For a long history of the Adages, Drummond, i. 271–306. Jortin is also still interesting, and gives quotations.

afterwards they went together to Rome. His Italian sojourn had been a nicely balanced conflict between bodily fare which he thought disagreeable as well as meagre, and scholarly charms which at last centred in Rome. There he was made much of, and it would have been easy for him, as for many others, to make it his home. But, had he done so, the result would probably have been a loss to scholarship: his reputation might have spread, but his output would have been less. And England, where Henry VIII seemed likely to become a scholar's king, was more than beckoning to him.

In the end, however, the promises of Italian help remained mere promises, and the discomforts of the journey back, with the oppressive stoves in the inns, with the mixed company in them, and with more than a suspicion of garlic, remained to the fastidious scholar a horrible memory, revealed in the *Colloquies*. It was on the return journey, moving towards his friend More in England, that he planned the *Encomium Moriae*, which was written in a week[1] after his arrival (1509). In Italy he had added somewhat to the Greek which he had learnt both at Oxford and by himself, and he had also received the hall-mark of a doctor's degree from the university of Turin.[2] It was small wonder that his fellow monks at Steyn should urge such a celebrated brother to return to their fold. But brighter and more congenial prospects were now opening before him: "mountains of gold were offered" him, and at a later date he says he could not have lived had it not been for the help so freely sent from England.[3] Scholars there seemed to have come to their own, for Henry VIII, who when a boy had challenged Erasmus to prove his powers, was now the king, and under his smile earning seemed likely to flourish. From Louvain almost

[1] See Nichols, ii. 5; Allen, i. 459 and ii. 94.

[2] Not Bologna: see Nolhac, *Érasme en Italie*, pp. 9–10; Nichols, i. 24, 28, and 417.

[3] On Erasmus's degree at Cambridge, into which the late Dr. Searle of Queens' College made researches, see Allen, vol. i, app. vi.

F　　　　65

alone came a murmur against the *Praise of Folly*,[1] the success
of which indeed surprised its author most of all; the very
highest dignitaries of the Church were pleased with it, and
we need not suppose its appearance would have been a bar
to its author's promotion; some of the monks, the "obscure
men" who were later on to attack Reuchlin, might dislike
what they understood of it, and to them its elegant Latinity
was of itself suspicious.

To this time belongs, not, it is true, the first, but a stronger
impulse towards theology and, along with it, towards
teaching. Nothing is worth doing, he says, except theology,
and, in his letters of this period, teaching appears as a most
honourable work. The paganism of Italy had disgusted
him although its classic glamour had so strongly drawn him.
If the *Novum Instrumentum*, the great biblical work of
Erasmus, did not appear until much later, the copy of a
manuscript made by Peter Meghen[2] (the one-eyed carrier,
the Cyclops of the letters) is dated 1506–9, so that the work
itself was thought of and in process at an early date. His
collation of the New Testament was now finished and his
St. Jerome (including the Pseudo-Jerome on St. Paul's Epistles, really due to Pelagius) well on the way. This fresh impulse towards biblical work was due not only to his friendship with Colet and to that deepening of early tendencies
which so often happens in middle age, but also to his Italian
journey and his association with the press at Venice. He had
seen how much was possible, and the scholar of the study
was on the way to becoming the author of the busy world,
independent of the patrons who helped him so grudgingly.[3]

[1] There was a little mystification about the *Praise of Folly*, as there
was in a greater degree about the *Julius Exclusus*. The work was taken
to Paris and printed (Erasmus says) from a faulty manuscript. But he
seems to have taken it there himself (Nichols, ii. 16).

[2] See Allen, ii. 181–4, and also 164–6.

[3] His search for patrons still continued, as can be seen, for instance, in
some letters printed in Nichols's vol. iii, but the need for them is less
irksome and more incidental than at first.

His sojourn at Cambridge is perhaps known to some through his complaints about the small beer and the bad wine. His own excuse was that his old enemy the stone (fatal to so many medieval scholars) necessitated wine of a special kind. It was Greek, and his friend Andreas Ammonius was to procure it, and payment was promised even beforehand. It may be noticed that the same scandal flourished even more in the hot-house air of Italy, where Erasmus was depicted working double tides at the Aldine Press and drinking more than double. But it is only a scandalous story, and to clear the memory of Erasmus it is only necessary to say that the wine was sweetened with liquorice. His stay at Cambridge, where he was Lady Margaret Reader, lasted from 1511 to 1514; the university was but a poor patron, and part of the time the plague, which he mentions so often and with such fear in his letters to his friend Gunnell,[1] was rife and the undergraduates, few in number to begin with, were frightened away. He had been promised thirty nobles as stipend, and to raise this sum public help had to be asked for; an appeal was made by the university to the liberality of Mountjoy.[2] In his last six months at Cambridge Erasmus spent sixty nobles, and received from his hearers only one. But at Cambridge, where Bishop Fisher and the foundation of the Lady Margaret had already done something for sound theology and for training in pastoral work, Erasmus was in an atmosphere suited to himself, and letters such as those of Henry Bullock[3] of Queens', where Erasmus stayed, proved that his sojourn was to be fruitful for the future. It is very probable that Tindale was attracted to Cambridge by the teaching of the great scholar, and the biblical tendency which was so strong

[1] Allen, i. 550, 561; Nichols, ii. 117, 132.
[2] The letter (probably of the date 1512) is printed in Nichols, vol. ii. 73, app. A, p. 613, and in Allen, i. 613.
[3] See Allen, vol. iii, Ep. 826. See also Mullinger, *History of the University of Cambridge*. Bullock afterwards presided at the Cambridge burning of Luther's works in 1521 (Mullinger, i. 571).

in the English Reformation was, in all likelihood, due to Erasmus and his work. His *Paraphrases* were afterwards ordered to be placed in English churches; and we may remember the Bible study of the little group at the White Horse,[1] some of whom became famous in later days and some of whom passed to Wolsey's foundation at Oxford.

In July 1514 Cambridge and London were left for Basle, to which he travelled by way of Flanders, reaching the home of the Amorbachs and Froben in August, and it is now that the central part of his life begins. At Basle he made many friends, not only the great printers but their readers (as we should call them now), and above all Beatus Rhenanus. His appointment as counsellor to Prince Charles (afterwards emperor) and the invitation to take up his abode in the Netherlands was an honour due to his renown. In March 1515 he returned to England, but in June of that year he paid another visit to Basle. In 1516 his New Testament with Latin translation and notes appeared, about which a pretty quarrel raised by Stunica in Spain and by Edward Lee (afterwards Archbishop of York) in England raged for some time. The work was the application of sound learning and the critical method to theology. His critical work would not perhaps be highly rated now, but his exegesis was always reverent and sometimes new. The novelties, however, when seized upon by those who had not the writer's own regard for the authority of the Church, were sometimes dangerously used. His discussion of our Lord's treatment of divorce, for instance, fitted in too well with the licence of the day not to be carried further, and much of later discussion may be put down to their influence.[2] For instance in Exeter diocese

[1] *Cambridge History of English Literature*, iii. 37. Milman (*Latin Christianity*, ix. 346) has a brief but good statement of the importance of the *Paraphrases*.

[2] See the evidence I gave quoting opinions of continental divines upon divorce, in the *Report of the Royal Commission upon Divorce*, *Minutes of Evidence*, iii. 283 f. The copy of Erasmus's tractate on

Bishop Alley found some malcontents who denied the descent of Christ into Hades, and their opinions, he says, "they ground upon Erasmus and the Germans in the first place even if more especially upon the authority of Mr. Calvin and Mr. Bullinger."[1] But there was solid work and reverent love of the gospel in the work, and it did not fail of its result. Erasmus was its author, but the method he followed and the spirit in which he wrote were alike those of his early teachers, the pious and laborious Brethren of the Common Life. And so the dying Middle Ages were linked by their greatest product to the foundation of the Reformation age itself.

In August 1516 Erasmus left England for the Continent; Calais, Antwerp, Brussels, Antwerp again, received him; a short trip to England in March and April in 1517, during which he visited Rochester, brought him again to his most congenial friends: in May and June he passed over again to Antwerp (the home of the court), and in July 1517 he settled at Louvain, surrounded by his beloved books and all his belongings. Here he made his home, with occasional moves to Antwerp and a longer journey to Basle for the purpose of editing his most important works (May to August 1518). Then he returned to Louvain; illness met him on the way and made him wish for rest, which was, however, denied him by controversies and fear of attacks more or less malicious. Erasmus describes the journey[2] in a letter to the deservedly loved Beatus Rhenanus. A journey in Germany was not at all to the taste of the writer and discomforts were many. But at Boppard he was welcomed by the toll-collector, who knew his works and his fame: he was ready to

---

Marriage which he presented to Catherine of Aragon is in Emmanuel College Library.

[1] See Strype, *Annals* (Oxford ed., 1824), vol. i, pt. i, p. 519. For the reference I am indebted to Dr. Gibson's *Thirty-Nine Articles*, i. 161.

[2] Ep. 867 to Beatus Rhenanus, *c*. 15 Oct. 1518. Allen's introductory note Ep. iii, p. 392 discusses the route.

charge no toll to the sailors who had conveyed such a precious freight: he sent them two bottles of wine and then more still when they begged for it: Erasmus himself he was proud to entertain in his own house. The little story shows how the scholar's fame had spread, and it gave him innocent pleasure, as we can see from his account. Henceforth his health caused him more real anxiety and increased his fastidiousness. But by this time the Lutheran tragedy had begun its tumultuous course, sometimes rapid, sometimes slow, but always full of discord and disturbance.

Louvain itself reflected the movement of the busier world outside. It was the home of conservatism, which should not always be interpreted as obscurantism, for there were also better tendencies of thought to be reckoned with. It was the time when the professorships of the Three Languages were founded to the glory and the gain of the great university, which from time to time, and not least in these most modern days, has drawn to itself the attention of the world. Hebrew, Greek, and Latin studied with the newer zeal were called to the help of the older modes of thought. In this academic venture, which was made possible by private liberality, Erasmus took the deepest interest, and his letters are filled with inquiries about suitable candidates. Strangely enough, Hebrew was the chair most easily filled; for Greek and Latin it was rightly thought most essential that experts capable of teaching conversation should be found. Languages treated as dead tended, it was felt, to become really so to those who studied them. Hitherto Latin had been a living tongue, and by its great unity of thought and literature had bound into one those who gave themselves up to their inspiration. But with the Reformation there came a great cleavage of thought, and some of the newer school gradually ceased to use the old material embodied in patristic, scholastic, and legal literature. For some generations indeed it was freely used. Reformers, like Melanchthon and Beza on the Continent and like Cranmer and Jewel in England, founded their thought and arguments upon authorities and collections which were used by their opponents also. Then theological schools of opinion based upon allegiance to party leaders split off from each other. These schools soon came to prefer the spirit of their own day to the authoritative tradition of older systems, and barriers of local limits shut off rising generations from the once common ground of ancient and medieval learning. But for some time the common study of the ancient tongues delayed the change. German reformers cherished them, to begin with, because they, like Melanchthon, had grown up in the atmosphere of the Renaissance. In the opposite camp the Jesuits, who were led by the solid learning of Lanez, were for one or two generations under influences much the same.[1] But the gradual loss of a common language and the growing disuse of common material shook the solid ground upon which common schools had once stood together. Men ceased to think or read in common, and tendencies of all kinds pushed them apart.

All this was to be seen most plainly on the Continent; in England things were a little different, and the great Caroline divines are found using the old material and entering freely into the heritage of the past. Because they did so, they seemed to many in their own day to be reactionary and out of sympathy with the world around them; but just because they did so, they possessed a solidity of thought and a continuity of tradition which make the study of them most valuable for us to-day. This revolution of thought on a large scale was completed everywhere before the Reformation was two centuries old; medieval learning, medieval ways of thought were slowly lost, and the Middle Ages themselves seemed useless and far away. Medieval Latin was cast aside like an ancient and discarded dress: it has been left

[1] The educational changes which gather around the *Ratio Studiorum* and its history illustrate the change. The changing opinions about Erasmus are seen in the curious variations about his works in the index: see G. H. Putnam, *The Censorship of the Church of Rome*, i. 196 f. and 225; i. 338 f.; ii. 14.

for our own generation to disinter medieval thought, and through endeavours at understanding the Middle Ages, to restore the continuity which the Reformation, even more by its change of education than by its new theology, had unhappily destroyed. The Trilingual College at Louvain, and such new foundations sharing the spirit of the past, had, therefore, an influence and a significance entirely their own. Unhappily, both those who might have supported them from the inside but did not, and those who attacked them from outside, hindered their full fruition. So the foundation over which Erasmus watched with such loving care did not achieve all that it might. It remained a model for other universities to copy, but at Louvain itself there were theologians who looked on it with suspicion, and the course of politics, civil and ecclesiastical, denied it the international importance it should have gained. At Louvain,[1] then, Erasmus found himself in the future stronghold of the Counter-Reformation; incidentally, too, he came into closer touch with Ulric von Hutten who represented those sides of the German Renaissance and Reformation with which he himself was least in sympathy,[2] whom he met at Mainz in 1514[3] and some three years later at Frankfort. With the death of Colet in 1519, and with the growing ferment in Germany, he seems to be losing friends of his own standing, some by death and others more sadly by division; he is drawn into new connections, and from 1518 onwards his relations to leaders like Luther and Hutten are increasingly important.

Little need be said about the attitude of Erasmus towards admitted abuses: his *Colloquies* and the *Praise of Folly* are

[1] "I heard a camel preach at Louvain, that we should have nothing to do with anything that is new": Canonisation of John Reuchlin in *Colloquies*.

[2] For a discussion of later relations between Erasmus and Hutten, see Strauss, *Life of Ulric von Hutten*, pp. 58, 172, 211, 324 f., and 355 (Eng. translation by Mrs. G. Sturge, 1874).

[3] Allen, ii. 4, n. 12; also Ep. 365 (ii. 155 f.); Nichols, ii. 154.

evidence enough in themselves. The important point is that amid the rising uproar everything he denoted by his expression "good letters" seemed to be at stake. In his letters he writes more than once that he was never "a teacher of error or a leader of riot."[1] On the positive side it became evident that while ready freely to criticise even a pope (if he did write *Julius Exclusus*[2] he was none the less a little ready to avoid owning it as his offspring), he yet held the Papacy to be the centre of unity and a possible source of reform. His own favourite methods were calm and quiet; new disturbances he feared to excite, for they so often turned out contrary to expectation.

Nevertheless, he was ready to use satire: it was first cousin to his peculiar humour. Thus, for instance, a Spanish Observant attacked him and pleaded an attack of fever as an excuse for imperfections in his work. The mere title of the reply quietly disposed of such an antagonist: *Responsio adversus febricitantis cuiusdam libellum*. But satire backed up by a life like Hutten's was worse than useless, and so the two men parted company. Just as Erasmus differed from Hutten, so the *Colloquies* and *Praise of Folly* differed from the *Epistolae Obscurorum Virorum*. The latter, brilliant though it was, was purely literary; the former have a dominant ethical purpose. Erasmus, moreover, a citizen of the world but with no real home or fatherland of his own, failed to understand the national fire which, after all, burnt in the very words of the riotous knight he loathed. "Beata Tranquillitas" was not the motto of Mutianus Rufus alone. And yet so disturbed was the state of public opinion, so peculiar was the position of Erasmus himself, that he was suspected

---

[1] See Drummond, ii. 44, and a letter to Wolsey, Allen, iii. 587; Nichols, iii. 378.

[2] On the *Julius Exclusus* (the text of which is given in Jortin, ii. 600–22), see Nichols, ii. 299, 446–7, 495, 610 and 611; iii. 19, 20–1, 290, and especially 290. For a full discussion, see Allen, ii. 418 f. For an English translation, see Froude, 156 f.

on the one hand of writing the attack of Henry VIII upon Luther and, on the other hand, of writing Luther's reply.

Hutten, unlike Erasmus, welcomed revolution, both religious and political. The intercourse between the two men gradually became a trial of fence, the one seeking to involve the other while he was skilfully kept at bay. Hutten was anxious to draw Erasmus into his own circle, or at any rate to claim the credit of so great an ally; Erasmus, on the other hand, much as he had admired Hutten to begin with, was resolved to avoid entanglements only too likely to become discreditable. Hutten, moreover, showed himself somewhat unscrupulous; he printed without leave a letter from Erasmus to his patron, Albert of Mainz, in which he was spoken of favourably.[1] Then later on a bitter attack by Hutten upon Archbishop Lee, who had criticised the *Novum Instrumentum*, did not fit the great scholar's idea of controversy. Hutten tried to frighten[2] Erasmus into a wholehearted advocacy of Lutheranism and was particularly displeased with a letter to Laurinus (1523) defining the Erasmian position in the Lutheran controversies.[3] On the other side Erasmus wrote to Hutten (from Antwerp, although Louvain was his head-quarters) sending him a charming portrait of More and begging him to keep himself for the service of the Muses, for which he was so apt.[4] Thus the relations of the two men drifted inevitably from bad to worse, until they reached a crisis in the miserable visit of Hutten to Basle (1522). Here he tried repeatedly to see Erasmus, but was

---

[1] Strauss, *Ulric von Hutten*, p. 320. The account of the whole matter in Drummond, vol. ii, ch. xiv, is fair and full.

[2] Strauss, p. 325.   [3] Ep. 650.

[4] Strauss, p. 172. For the portrait of More, Nichols, iii. 387 f. Writing to Bude from Louvain (22 Feb. 1518) Erasmus says: "I am truly glad that you like Hutten as I was myself singularly delighted with the man's character": Nichols, iii. 260. Eppendorf, Hutten's executor, really tried to blackmail Erasmus and caused him not only annoyance but even alarm.

carefully thwarted by the conditions his expected host placed upon the interview. The whole incident was as painful as it was perhaps inevitable. Erasmus, with his just dislike to the public policy and the private life of Hutten, was not to be drawn like Zwingli,[1] to whom he dedicated his *Spongia*, his spirited defence, into a patronage certain to be discreditable to the patron.[2]

In 1521 his old schoolfellow at Deventer, who was also a former professor of Louvain, became Pope as Adrian VI, and for a time hopes of reform seemed likely to be realised. He was invited to Rome, but did not go, although he gave his advice as to what should be done.[3] A council was necessary: everyone must give up something for the common good. The evil had gone too far for burning or amputation. To consider all the questions which had arisen there should be called together from every country men of uncorrupted integrity, grave, mild, and without passion, whose opinion—— But at this point the letter to the short-lived Pope breaks off suddenly and remains a most curious field for conjecture. The meeting of such a council was retarded by violence and stupidity on the side of the monks who had attacked Reuchlin, by violence and impatience on the side of Luther and his followers. Once Erasmus wrote of Luther that he seemed raised up divinely for the reformation of manners; at another time he said the monks were thirsting

---

[1] Extracts from the *Spongia* are given in Jortin, ii. 277–9. For Zwingli's reception of Hutten see Stähelin's *Huldreich Zwingli* (Basel, 1895), ii. 314 f., and Jackson's *H. Zwingli* (*Heroes of the Reformation*, 1910). Zwingli was not only a thoroughgoing humanist like Hutten, but was himself concerned in political schemes for a league of cities, something like the revolutionary schemes of Hutten. Hence he, unlike Erasmus, was doubly in sympathy with him.

[2] On the whole the opinion of Erasmus about Hutten is best expressed by his words to Jodocus Jonas in Ep. 572 (Le Clerc) of the year 1521: "the more I have loved the genius and the talents of Hutten, the more concerned I am to lose him by these troubles."

[3] See Epp. 649, 793, and part ii (App.), 321, *c.* 1700 (Le Clerc); also 632, 633, 639, 641, and 648.

for his blood, and that he himself for his part cared not whether they ate him boiled or roast.

It is significant to notice that, when the point of Papal supremacy had been clearly raised by the controversies with Hutten and Luther, when Erasmus had given his opinion on the same side as More, and when the Lutheran movement was fairly under way, the first large edition of the *Familiar Colloquies* appeared (1522).[1] The point of view shown in them is the same as Erasmus had already taken, and the publication at that precise time is proof enough that Erasmus had little of the timidity so often ascribed to him. Unflinching love of truth, together with a deep hatred of violence, which he held contrary to the law of Christ, were his great characteristics. But he had a mind singularly detached, and thus his attitude pleased neither side. A detached mind, like a detached lady, is an extremely awkward travelling companion, and for a monk seemed to verge upon the improper.

On 14 September 1523 Adrian VI died. The character of his successor, Clement VII, sent by Erasmus to Christopher, the reforming bishop of Basle, is significant. He expected that the emperor and cardinals would help the new Pope to re-establish the now shrunken power of the Papacy. Then his successor, who must in the course of things follow soon, would manage things as he pleased. The next year, while Erasmus was suffering from illness and the attacks of his widely-spread foes, Tunstall and friends at Rome urged him to write against Luther, whom even so late as 1527 he described to Albert of Carpi as "a good man divinely sent," and at last (1524) he does so. But the point he chooses for attack is to be noted. He wrote upon Free-will.

The choice of this topic is sometimes explained by saying that Erasmus deliberately picked upon an admittedly minor point because, while his real sympathies were with Luther, he yet feared to take his side although he would not act

[1] A small edition had appeared in 1519, but this was much larger. See Drummond, ii. 151.

against him. He made a demonstration, it is said, with as little violence to his own principles as possible. But, after all, this very point was an essential part of the Erasmian theology.[1] Mr. Seebohm has already dealt with the matter and shown as much. Luther to the end was scholastic in his methods, although he owed more to Erfurt with its traditions of scriptural study[2] than is often supposed. Erasmus, on the other hand, postulated the free and full development of the individual, trained and disciplined, as the very foundation of theology. Hence his choice of a subject for controversy, the importance of which was to be shown by the future history of reformed doctrine. Free-will was to play a more important part in later days than was as yet foreseen. Calvin had not arisen although Luther had long been active. But Erasmus was gifted with a further vision.

A letter to Fisher of Rochester (4 September 1524), after incidentally urging upon him the evils of glass and bricks and mortar compared to wooden floors and walls, summarised the theological situation as Erasmus saw it.

> You congratulate me upon my triumph. How I triumph I do not know, for of a surety I am maintaining a threefold war, with these Roman pagans who are jealous of me, with certain theologians and monks who are turning every stone to destroy me, and with some rabid Lutherans who roar at me because it is I alone, they say, who stay their victory. I do so because I do not choose at risk of life to swallow the whole creed of Luther, in which there is much I do not understand, much that I am doubtful of, much that even if it were safe, I should not care for conscience' sake to profess.[3]

So far the theological side of Erasmus's activity has only been dealt with incidentally. From first to last he took his stand upon "sound letters." Here he used the vast stores of

---

[1] It was also more fundamental with Luther than is sometimes thought. See Grisar, *Luther*, i. 43 f. and 117 f. (Eng. translations).

[2] For these traditions, see Albert, *Matthias Doering* (Stuttgart, 1892), p. 17; N. Paulus, *Der Augustiner Bartholomäus Arnoldi von Usingen* (Strassburg, 1893), p. 5, n. 2; also Ullmann, *Reformers before the Reformation*, i. 218 f.   [3] See Ep. 698.

primitive and patristic learning, thus laying a sure foundation for future ages; but he also made full use of the new learning and new ways of study, linguistic and educational, which had lately come into play. Two tendencies of thought and work are always to be found, and there are always men who give themselves over solely to one of them. If they are content merely to keep what has been handed down, they fail to be in touch with their own day: they are not only branded as reactionary but tend to become so in reality. If, on the other hand, they look solely at their own day and give themselves up to its tendencies they miss that continuity of thought and work with the past which is necessary for permanent progress. The "spirit of the day" too often gives such a man a delusive impression of influence, while all the time he runs the risk of dissipating his power and losing his control of the future. Both these dangers were escaped by Erasmus. He was reviled alike by reactionaries and revolutionaries. But the lines of educational work laid down by him were followed in the next century by the best teachers in both theological camps, and exactly the same was the case with his theology. The "mediating theologians," Contarini, Pflug, Gropper, and among rather later Lutherans, Cassander, may be held his real successors so far as the doctrine of divine grace is concerned. Luther under-estimated the value of good works: although it was only in his later years that he asserted salvation by faith alone with full emphasis on the qualification "alone," yet he had the germ of this belief in earlier years, certainly in 1516. Erasmus, on the other hand, laid stress upon the freedom of man's will and upon the necessity of good works. A life of righteousness was, with him, the first condition. With Luther, righteousness was fundamentally a theological expression, a part of thoelogy and not of life. And the explanation of this fundamental difference is to be found in the differing conceptions the two men had of the Church. Luther really cared little for the Church, for its organisation and its resulting effect upon life. Erasmus, on the other hand, looked upon it as the earthly sphere in which man lived and where he came into vital touch with God. Here Erasmus, the scholar, was practical, while Luther, who, in the end, worked a revolution in life, was theoretical. But the difference prevented the two from working together.

Writing to John Lang, his friend of early Erfurt and Wittenberg days, Luther spoke of "our Erasmus" (1517).[1] The name of Erasmus was a fashionable one in all universities, and Luther, like all students, had come under its fascination. Moreover, he looked with pleasure at the attack made by Erasmus upon abuses of all kinds, and he welcomed his ridicule of ignorance among monks. But even thus early Luther saw by instinct that he and Erasmus were certain to go different ways; through their common correspondent, Spalatin, he urged Erasmus to emphasise St. Paul's apparent condemnation of the righteousness of works. And he was eager to point out (in a way more significant than tactful) that to be a good scholar was very different from being a good Christian. In other words Luther was something of a mystic, and inclined, like Wyclif before him and many other revivalists after him, to underrate human learning. If towards the end of the sixteenth century we find the Lutherans deserting the traditions of humanism for a kind of Lutheran scholasticism, neglecting scholarship for theology of an abstract kind, they were in reality only following where Luther had pointed out the way. But Erasmus regarded "sound learning" as an essential of Christian progress, and if there was to be learning and scholarship, the freedom of man to work and to think was also essential. When Erasmus and Luther, then, engaged in controversy on the slavery of the will the dispute was about the fundamentals of their respective schemes. And the later history of Lutheranism justified the line taken by Erasmus.

Critics of Erasmus, notably Seebohm and Drummond,

[1] See Grisar *Luther*, i. 43.

and later Preserved Smith, have described Erasmus as an anti-dogmatist, although Drummond is inclined to hold him an Arian.[1] But the passages quoted in defence of this charge have been shown by a rigid and acute Scottish theologian to be almost identical in phrase with passages in the thoroughly orthodox Waterland,[2] so that the argument may be dismissed. The other view that he was essentially anti-dogmatic and anticipated the more "modern spirit" has more to support it and needs examination. It is clear, to begin with, that Erasmus always keeps his theology in close touch with life; he never regards any theological debate or conclusion as purely abstract and he always handles it reverently. But he shows an openness of inquiry, a readiness to discuss, which sometimes leads modern readers, as it led men of his own day, to suppose that he regarded many questions as open and that he meant his speculation to be destructive. So we find Bishop Fisher in his own day disliking the *Colloquies*[3] and leading the English condemnation of them; in modern days we find Seebohm praising Erasmus for the very same reasons. And in the "Ichthyophagia," to take the longest and most considerable of the *Colloquies*, there is much to justify Bishop Fisher and Mr. Seebohm. The characters, the fishmonger and the butcher, although Erasmus had not, I think, the dramatic gift, are learned beyond their tribe, brilliant and acute in their suggestions and in an unrestrained pursuit of them, seeming to go far in their freedom and to reach extreme conclusions. We may suppose that the fishmonger, who accounted for his theological learning by the fact that he often dined with his Dominican customers, must often have shocked his hosts, and we can understand

[1] Drummond, ii. 162.

[2] Dr. Marcus Dods in *Erasmus and other Essays*, p. 55. This writer does full justice to the manliness of thought always found in Erasmus (p. 25) and makes a good defence for him against the charge of hurried critical work on the New Testament. But the press correctors were far behind our own University Press readers.

[3] See Erasmus's reply, Ep. 974.

why Farel, "the ignorant ranter" as Erasmus called him, was surprised, after a debate with him on the Invocation of Saints,[1] at the difference in their belief and practice.

But even here Erasmus was medieval; he was following the usage of the greater schoolmen and of medieval university teachers; like them he thought and speculated freely, following trains of argument whither they led. The later scholastics, those of his own day, were no longer speculative, but merely repeated ancient knowledge and old discussions; the reformers were well on the way to an equally traditional scholasticism of their own. But we ought not to take Erasmus's treatment of his themes either as mere literary business or as deliberately destructive. He was following the method of medieval teachers and using their freedom, although the method which had been so successful in olden lecture-rooms might have its risks in more modern market-places, where its rules and its intentions were not always understood. And like the medieval teachers Erasmus never forgot the voice of authority which spoke to him when his discussions and digressions had ended. Here, I think, we have the explanation why he wrote as he did and yet complained that he was misunderstood alike by reformers who hailed him as their own and by the rigidly orthodox who held him destructive. He might satirise the schoolmen of his own day, but nevertheless he thought boldly but reverently, as had the schoolmen of earlier days. But in his time methods of thought and even thought itself were hardening. So he was misunderstood then by men of opposite schools, just as he is misunderstood now when he is hailed as a herald of modern thought.[2]

[1] Ep. 707.

[2] He says in his treatise on Free-will (Op. ix. 1215 D): "I have such a horror of dogmatism, that I could easily declare myself a member of the sceptic school, whenever I am not met by the inviolable authority of Holy Scripture and of the Church, to which I willingly submit my reason in all things, whether I understand what it prescribes or do not understand" (see Drummond, ii. 361). This is perfectly clear. And the

Nothing caused Erasmus more pain than to be charged with heresy or even with a leaning towards it. And this was because he was so sure of his own full acceptance of the Church's teaching. Thus his controversy with Bedda[1] (in 1525) at Paris took up much time which he would fain have spent otherwise, and this was not solely because of the danger it might bring upon him. So, too, the charge of unsound teaching about Christ brought against him by Lefèvre, whom he respected even when forced to oppose him, was a great pain to him. And his letters are ample proof of this:[2] he was horrified to think that anyone could suppose he had taught wrongly upon the two natures in Christ. And accordingly he took great, perhaps unnecessary, pains to defend himself—not from timidity, for he never hesitated to speak his mind, but because he valued the truth.

More and more revolutionary became the times: in 1524 the Peasants' Revolution surged round the cities, and the controversies round Erasmus raged as keenly down to 1529. At length (1525) the *Colloquies* were condemned by the Sorbonne, although Francis I did stay the wearisome Bedda from buzzing round Erasmus. But one strange result of the condemnation was that as soon as it had become widely known one bookseller ordered 24,000 copies and disposed of them. In Spain, in France, and nearer home (which now meant Basle, whither Erasmus had betaken himself in 1521) where the tide of Lutheranism was rising, under the leadership of Farel (an agitator whom Erasmus never liked) and of Oecolampadius, an old friend whom he respected,[3] everywhere raged strife and controversy. And the old dispute

---

scepticism of Erasmus was, as it seems to me, far more akin to that of medieval scholastics, who were inspired by eagerness not by doubt, than to that of more modern writers.

[1] Drummond, vol. ii, ch. xvi, describes the whole controversy at length.   [2] See Nichols, iii. 177, 179, 184, and 187.

[3] Oecolampadius had been a press corrector at Basle and had been in charge of the Greek text of the *Novum Instrumentum* (Nichols, ii. 217, 534, and iii. 310).

with Hutten, who had died (August 1526) in poverty and sadness, dragged on its way with a weary tag of a quarrel and a threatened law-suit with Eppendorf only appeased by the dedication of a book to him.

Much has been written about the unpleasant search for patrons and patrons' gifts in the letters. This is strongly marked in the earlier years, and in days before writers were brought face to face with a large public through the agency of the printing-press it was common: the dedications to patrons and the search to find easy victims of this kind have long since been replaced by a Note—"To the Reader"—or the more terrific descriptions of works on the coloured wrapper. But as Erasmus found steadfast friends, as he became almost supreme in the world of letters, and something of a figure in the larger world of politics, "the begging letters" disappear.

From the early period we pass to later days. With a letter of 2 July, 1525, we begin a long series of forty-three letters from Erasmus to Erasmus Schets, a banker at Antwerp.[1] Schets is said to have come to Antwerp from Maestricht, and then became a banker and merchant: he married the daughter of a citizen of the same prosperous class: he visited King Manuel of Portugal and entertained Charles V at his house. He introduced himself by letter to his great and admired namesake, when some Spanish friends gave him letters for forwarding to Erasmus, availing themselves of the safer facilities enjoyed by bankers: in sending the parcel he gave free rein to his admiration for the scholar. Erasmus saw that here was a man of taste and worthy of trust. Their friendship grew: he became an adviser in matters of finance, but he long survived his friend, dying 13 May, 1550. The friendship between the two Erasmi is much like what often exists in these days between a great writer and his banker or his publisher. But it is pleasant to see Erasmus at rest and peace,

[2] See Allen vi, Appendix VII and note to Ep. 1541. Schets's first letter is Ep. 1583.

sure of his position and a man of note, a dictator in his peculiar sphere whom even religious controversies or political revolutions could hardly shake. The days when help had to be asked for and money sought for at the price of some self-respect were over. His religious faith had grown deeper and filled his soul: he could look on much work done for the Kingdom of God and the Faith of Christ, which were now stronger through the sacred learning he had loved so greatly and laboured for so long.

In 1527 Froben the elder died just after the edition of St. Augustine had begun to appear, a worthy continuation of editions of St. Jerome, St. Cyprian, and part of St. Athanasius. Soon the Reformation passed into its acutest stage, the discussion upon the Eucharist; and before the works of St. Augustine had all appeared (1529), Erasmus had moved to the beautiful city of Freiburg in the Breisgau, with its impressive cathedral dominating the picturesque market square. At Basle he had contrived to stay for a time the sale of a book by Oecolampadius written in a Zwinglian tone. But by 1529 the tide of change rose higher: the mass was abolished and the images removed from the churches. Sadly, therefore, he left the city which he had learnt to love and which still seems to speak of him more perhaps than any other place except the Cambridge cloisters of Queens'. Sadly enough he left it; neither in England nor in Bohemia, although both invited him, did he choose to live; he wished to stay in the Emperor's lands (he was, we may remember, an imperial councillor), and at Freiburg his wish was gratified.

In spite of his continued activity in letters, his life was now practically at an end, for labours like his demanded a more peaceful atmosphere. Illness prevented him from attending as an imperial councillor the council at Augsburg in 1530, and although the accession of Paul III (1534) gave the world a Pope wishful of reform, the ideal of a council to bring about unity was merely a dream. His old friends, too, were leaving him alone in a world rapidly growing strange: Warham and Pirckheimer, the typical burgher of the great city of Nuremberg, gentle deaths removed; Fisher and More deaths that were cruel and violent. In 1535 he left Freiburg and went to Basle, his beloved home of old, as a resting-place on the way to some spot where the "beata tranquillitas" might be his. There and then he wrote his *Ecclesiastes*, a tractate on preaching, and was preparing for the press a new edition of his letters, many of which had been pirated and published here and there. On 28 June, 1536, he wrote his last letter, the end of a long and magnificent series which is almost a history of the theology and scholarship, of the theologians and writers, of a great and momentous time. And on 12 July he passed away.

He left, if I can read his letters right, a world which he did not fully understand, and for which he had no longer the hopes of old. It was no longer the old world of universal scholarship with a public opinion which was that of learned men, which was really the same in every land and centred in the colleges and schools. It was hardly the world of the living Latinity he had loved and tried to teach, although a few Ciceronians might survive, even after the gentle ridicule he had directed at them. It was the world of Luther's German, of Cranmer's English, and Calvin's French.[1] The Vulgate, as a bond of union, he himself had in some ways helped to destroy; the national Bibles which superseded it spoke but feebly to the scholar of no fatherland in particular, much as he wished the Bible to become a well-known book. But he looked to the Greek of the Apostles enshrining the words of his Master Christ; among the strange interpretations of the day, some of them new and some of them old, with politics taking new shapes and doctrines presenting themselves in new forms, his tolerant, comprehensive, and

---

[1] The *Institution Chrestienne*, the French version of the *Christianae Religionis Institutio* (1536), was published in 1541. See Tilley, *Literature of the French Renaissance*, i. 227.

practical religion was acceptable to few. All could use his labours, Jesuits of the second generation and reformers of the extremist wing; but few would take his point of view. It was not Lutherans alone, but the leaders of the Counter-Reformation also, who were the real inheritors of his labours. If protestantism profited greatly by them, so did the revivified catholicism of the years after Trent.

Formed, as I take it, by the medieval world with its universal brotherhood of learning and of religion, he was loath to see it rent on the one hand by doctrinal divisions, on the other by the force of national life. And yet in many respects he was essentially modern, modern most obviously and to all in his humour; this was a gift which did not tend to conciliate his enemies, yet none the less added greatly to his own enjoyment of life. But humour and breadth of view seemed almost out of place in that time of strife when the new was rising, sometimes abruptly and sometimes gradually, out of the old. He had, moreover, to face a problem which is often a difficulty for us ourselves, how to combine the claim of authority and the rights of the individual.[1] And his success lay in this one great thing, that no man ever paid greater respect to the many-sided authority of the rich religious past, and yet at the same time was ever more truly himself—himself in the personality which he revealed to the world, in the special work which he undertook and the rich ability with which he wrought it to the end.[2] But to con-

[1] "There is no mean between authority and reason. . . . The *via media* belongs rightly to practice, not to speculation": *Life and Letters of F. J. A. Hort*, i. 437. Protestants found fault with Erasmus for his respect to authority; papalists criticised him for his independence of thought. He possessed each and strove to preserve both; and he reconciled them consistently in the sphere of practice.

[2] Erasmus writes: "I am all alone, because I have never attached myself to any party, and never will so long as God preserves my understanding": Ep. 1224 (a. 1532). And again he says he will be abundantly satisfied, if he himself satisfies good men, and above all, satisfies Christ (Ep. 1227). His boldness joined to reserve is seen in the "Inquiry concerning Truth" (*Colloquies*) where "he brings in the person of a

sider him as one who was a Lutheran at heart, and yet dared not to be such in deed, is surely wrong. From first to last he was the product and pupil of the Common Life, a scholar whose mind was not cast in the mould of Luther and was not cast in the mould of Leo. His was rather the mind of the more modern world, modern in its humour, modern in its gentleness, in its love of sound learning and of good letters. Yet modern as was his mind, he failed to estimate aright the new force of public opinion which the medieval world had not to reckon with. But he was the richest product of the older world. The paradox seems to suggest what our political philosophers and our religious leaders sometimes dare to hint, that either we are more medieval than we thought, or that the medieval world was more modern than we think.

Lutheran that there may be a more easy argeement betwixt them, in that they agree in the chief articles of the orthodox religion, although I have not added the remaining part of the inquiry, because of the nature of the times": Preface, a. 1526. In a letter to a Bohemian nobleman (Ep. 563) he says he accepts the Papal authority and thinks the Papacy entitled to respect, although he will not inquire how its authority has been gained. Here again we have that combination of respect for authority and of regard for private judgment which is so typical of Erasmus.

ESSAY III

LUTHER LITERATURE

SYNOPSIS

LUTHER LITERATURE

THAT excellent historian Wilhelm Maurenbrecher, who was thoroughly at home in the Reformation period and knew its Germany so well, wrote an Essay (No. VI) in his *Studien und Skizzen* on *Der Lutherliteratur*.[1] He showed how unsatisfactory the historical treatment of Luther up to that date had been. He did full justice to Ranke, who in this field of history, as in so many others, had lately begun a new epoch. And he also did justice to A. Ritschl, who had treated Luther's doctrine of Justification with an adequate knowledge of medieval theology and Scholasticism. Too often the current statement of the doctrine and the increasing importance given to it had led to a neglect of its historic setting and to varying views held about it.

Both historical and popular interest always fastens upon great events and great men. When we speak of Luther we think at once of events, great and dramatic in themselves, and of a personality equally great and equally fascinating. The first thirty years of the sixteenth century are absorbing in themselves, looked at alone and apart from earlier or from later times. A study of them is needed if we wish to understand the Middle Ages which formed them; it is needed as much if we wish to understand later ages which sprang out of them. In either case the personality of Luther looms so large that he must be understood if we would understand the Reformation: so large, indeed, that we are tempted, like others before us, to make the study of the Reformation mainly a study of him, of what he was and what he did.

For Germany and for Germans he meant so much that

[1] W. Maurenbrecher, *Studien und Skizzen* (Leipzig, 1874), pp. 207 seq.

91

this mistake was natural for them: they read their Bible in his vigorous German prose, and it had for them a power and a charm as great as had the prose of Cranmer for Englishmen. Germans could not escape from the influence of the great leader, whether they loved him or hated him. The Reformation dominated and divided German politics and German thought. And yet behind the great and widely held tradition there lay the riddle, as Lord Acton said, of "what made Luther?"

It was the great merit of Maurenbrecher to trace the growth of biographical Luther study: and his account is here summarised. Melanchthon, Luther's early friend and adviser (from early manhood onwards), who had stood by his side in many a crisis, who supplied a theological system which Luther lacked, who was, moreover, the real author of the Augsburg Apology (to use the name by which Luther at first called it), or the Confession as later days were to call it—Melanchthon was the first to write, as he had a right and even a duty to do, the first and the best life of his friend and fellow-labourer. Even in later days when he was accused of betraying the Lutheran theology through a wish for a wider unity and for the peace of God, he had to leave this wreath to lie supremely alone on Luther's grave.[1] Naturally it seemed to centre the Reformation in Luther and it therefore somewhat separated him from his fellows and his age. Then there followed the work of Sleidan,[2] the political historian of the Smalkaldic War, on the state of the Empire under Charles V: it was calm and largely theological, formulating even more impressively the Lutheran tradition, both personal and dogmatic. But Sleidan belonged to the second generations of Lutherans, and so

[1] *Vita Martini Lutheri* (Wittenberg, 1546). Reprinted by A. F. Neander: *Vitae Quattuor Reformatorum* (Luther, by Melanchthon, Melanchthon by Camerarius, Zwingli by Myconius and Calvin by Theodore Beza). Berlin 1841.

[2] Joh. Sleidanus: *De statu religionis et reipublicae Carolo V Caesare* (Strasbourg, 1555).

did not quite understand the storm and stress of the earlier times. And the theology of Luther's later years was described as that which, from the very first, the Reformers had tried to formulate. Then there followed Maimbourg[1] (1686), the learned French Jesuit, historian of heresies and much besides. To him replied Seckendorf.[2] The pair raised many contested issues, and in their discussion collected many documents. But controversy inevitably distorted the history of the movement, and along with it the life of Luther. Interest was quickened and dogmatic questions seemed to stand out as mattering most. The theology of Luther became for his followers something sacred. They thought, and in the end were convinced, that the doctrines for which Luther had stood must be identical with what they of that generation had come to believe. To them Justification by Faith was all-important, and so they read its pre-eminence and pre-existence into Luther's earlier days. Melanchthon might, as he said he did, meditate much on the Eucharist: questions about which, largely through the restless activity of Bucer, were much discussed from 1533 onwards, and conferences, such as that at Cassel in December (1534) and articles such as the Wittenberg Concord (1536) elaborated differences in attempting reconciliation. Incidentally the difference between Melanchthon and the body of Lutherans in their choice of doctrines explains something of the attacks by later Lutherans upon Melanchthon: he and they were taking different doctrinal paths. On the Roman side, moreover, the Tridentine position was taken as being of necessity identical with that of much earlier days. And, of course, they were ready to take Luther as being what and believing what his followers said he was and did. Dogmatic issues, somewhat distorted by mis-

---

[1] L. Maimbourg, *Histoire du Lutheranisme*, 1680.

[2] V. L. Seckendorf, *Commentarius historicus et apologeticus de Lutheranismo seu de reformatione religionis* (Frankfort, 1688). A German version by Frick with additions, 1714.

representations, were turned into battle-cries, and the past and the present were confused. It would seem, then, that critical studies of Luther's life, and of general Reformation history, should be treated, in the first place, separately if a satisfactory result were to be gained. Because this had not been done the study of Luther himself moved in a constant circle, and as it moved generated heat. Then, at length, came the historical revival of the nineteenth century.

Ranke was its foremost and greatest writer:[1] he went behind the material so often used: although not a professed archivist, he had an instinct for selecting decisive documents, and his views of men and events were always masterly. Even where he did not strike out new paths for himself, he often inspired others to do so. He brought the Lutheran tradition under the new modern historical study and examination, admirable in tone and feeling. A further step still remained to be taken and more than one influence worked to make this possible.

On the doctrinal side Albrecht Ritschl, in his well-known work on Justification,[1] put the medieval teaching about it in a fuller and fairer light: taking his results—and they could not easily be disproved—it would be easier to study Luther in his relations to both the general and special theology of the past by following his training. Would it be possible, after this was done, to treat Luther as marking a great break or a great step in the history of doctrine?

Passing from the theological to the purely historical

[1] It is a pleasure to refer to Dr. G. P. Gooch's *History and Historians of the Nineteenth Century* (London, 1913). Ch. vi. (pp. 96–102) deals with Ranke and gives a connected view of his works, as masterly in substance as it is wide in range.

[2] Albrecht Ritschl: *Die Christliche Lehre von der Rechtfertigung und Versöhnung* (3 vols., 1870: other editions since. An English translation by J. S. Black, Edinburgh, 1872, from the 3rd edition which is the same as the 4th, 1895). In Dr. A. E. Garvie: *The Ritschlian Theology* (Edinburgh, 1902) there are notes (pp. 398 and 400) on Recent English and German Literature.

side, we can see the same absorbing interest in Luther's great personality, and his dramatic life. A man who "lets himself go" will, as a rule, make a great impression, and Luther had that power.

Lutheran study, then, was gradually planning itself on larger lines and taking a newer shape, due to the new school of history. Many preliminary lines of research and many subsidiary were followed, and the number of really valuable books, some slight and some more ambitious, was great. The Bibliography was enlarged, and threatened to become over-powering.[1] A work referred to in the note below illustrates this.

But Adolf Harnack,[2] whose learning and acute judgment gave his considered views authority far beyond Germany, held that the study of theology should stop with Luther. He asserts that "the Reformation principle" laid down by Luther cancelled not only medieval doctrine, but also former Catholic presuppositions and dogma.[3]

This summary judgment appears to give Luther too

---

[1] There is a useful Bibliography which shows the number of works on Luther, *Thirty-five Years of Luther Research*, by J. M. Reu, D.D. (Chicago, 1917). It is very complete, up to date and most useful. There is a passage on Luther's health (pp. 96 *seq.*) which I should like to quote. "It is known that Luther was often ill during the thirties. It was Ebstein [*Dr. Martin Luthers Krankheiten und deren Einfluss auf seinen koerperlichen und geistigen Zustand*: 1908] who in 1908 dealt largely with it." He asserts that Luther suffered from calculi, constipation, piles, catarrh of the middle ear—almost deafness, periostitis, stomach affections, weakness of the heart, dysentery, cataract on one eye, and rheumatism. ". . . But he invariably rose above his sickness." He is often described as having a strong constitution, and he must indeed have needed it. The story of his last days is a pathetic record of weakness and sickness patiently borne or put aside for work held pressing.

[2] Adolf Harnack, *Lehrbuch der Dogmengeschichte*. [There are many editions: 4th edition, 3 vols., Tübingen, 1909–10; 6th edition, Freiburg im Breisgau, 1905 f.]. There is an English translation of the 3rd edition by N. Buchanan and others (7 vols., London, 1904–9).

[3] English translation, vol. vii. pp. 30 f. and 169.

commanding a seat in theological schools. To say this is not meant to lessen his historical importance in the world of action, but only to judge him as a theologian. If taken as true, it would deprive theological history of much vivid interest. For France, it would shut out the age of Pascal and Bossuet; for England, the Caroline divines, the Cambridge Platonists and later schools; for Germany we should put aside many individual scholars of great and varied learning; the whole field of modern Liturgical study would be smitten barren at a blow. Moreover Luther's knowledge of theology was neither extensive nor accurate.

F. Loofs,[1] a younger historian of doctrine (always to be studied with profit), puts the case differently. He thinks that the Reformation left many elements of medieval doctrine still in power, and therefore, that the history of doctrine must be carried beyond Luther. If we wish to put the Reformation in proper perspective, we must, I think, carry our connected study into later days: starting with the close of the Middle Ages, it should be treated as reaching from the beginning of the sixteenth century to the middle of the seventeenth. Political and territorial questions, inside Germany and outside it, found something of a settlement in the Treaty of Westphalia (1648). For England, the Restoration (1660) is the significant date. These seem to me the proper limits of the Reformation as a period of history. And theology moves and varies inside this field.

A difficulty for every part of history is found in disentangling amid its many elements the conservative and the revolutionary. In every age there are forces making for conservation and others making for change and sometimes even for revolution. As in the human body itself, there is a complicated struggle: at times one force is uppermost, at times the other; the judgment at any special moment

[1] F. Loofs, *Leitfaden zum studium der Dogmengeschichte* (2nd edition, enlarged, Halle, 1900).

is different from that for the final stage. Because of this changing and temporary appearance it is essential to look at any period from a safe distance, and not to let our critical eye confine itself to one selected spot, but range at leisure over the extended scene.

One of the most acute and stimulating German writers, Troeltsch, in defining the issue of the Reformation, has moved so far on the path of reaction as to see in the Anabaptists its truest children. He would agree, therefore, with Harnack in saying that Luther himself did not recognise the true issue of his movement and was not ready to follow to their logical end the principles from which he had started. But students of thought, like theologians, are too open to one-sided views, and need to be steadied by historians with a stricter taste, who wish, as Ranke put it, to describe "things as they really were."

On the whole the Protestant tradition held the field, but soon Catholic historians began to write challenging works of scholarship and force. In 1889 Johannes Janssen began to publish his *Geschichte des deutschen Volkes seit dem Ausgang des Mittelalter*: before his death (1891) he had reached the Thirty Years' War. By 1897, eighteen editions had come out. Pastor, who, in his *History of the Popes*, enriched by his studies of material in the Vatican Library, was to give us a more historic and less controversial spirit, superintended the later editions. Janssen aroused much controversy, but his work may be described in the words of Dr. G. P. Gooch[1] as "a corrective of Protestant tradition." Lutheran activity was naturally quickened, and many works, considerable biographies (such as Köstlin's) and special critical studies of great use appeared. And in 1882 the "Verein für Reformationsgeschichte" was founded, and happily it is at times difficult to tell from the books themselves whether the writers are Lutheran or Catholic.

[1] See G. P. Gooch, *History and Historians of the Nineteenth Century* (London, 1913), p. 562.

Thus the study of Luther was being planned on larger lines. He himself might still seem mysterious in his character and influence: descriptions, which aimed at epigram and only reached ambiguity, were common: "a typical German peasant" "one in whom the German race saw a type of itself," the latter being, as Lord Acton said, "a two-edged saying." The interest in Luther was great, but things were ready for a new stage.

Suddenly, and from an unexpected quarter, a bomb was thrown; its explosion brought about a new, and in some ways, a needed change.

In 1904 the great scholar and archivist, Heinrich Denifle, O.P., published his *Luther und Luthertum*, at the time when, along with Ehrle, the Librarian of the Vatican, he was travelling to England to take a well-deserved Honorary Degree at Cambridge:[1] some indignant Lutherans asked if the Cambridge Degree was to have been given for this attack on Luther. Articles on it and reviews were, of course, numerous, but here I only notice one in the *English Historical Review* by Dr. Figgis,[2] whose judgment was cautious and, of course, well-informed.

Denifle's reputation made any work of his most important. In particular his knowledge of European libraries and their MSS. was exhaustive, and he was sure to reach conclusions fresh, and either to be accepted or met with equal knowledge and power. It was easy to see at once that theological interests had drawn him to the work. So much for its

---

[1] H. Denifle, O.P., *Luther und Luthertum in der ersten Entwicklung Quellenmässig dargestellt* (Vol I., Mainz, 1904), second edition, pt. i., 1904; pt. ii. ed. A. M. Weiss, 1906. Appendix of quotations from St. Augustine down to Luther's day, *Die Abendländische Schriftausleger bis Luther über Justitia Dei* (Romans i. 17) *und Justificatio: Beitrag zur Geschichte der Literatur und des Dogmas im Mittelalter* (Mainz, 1906).

[2] E.H.R., vol. xxiii. p. 144.

substance: its spirit and taste were another matter. It was an attack of angry criticism which rose to virulence: Luther's truthfulness, and indeed his whole character, was attacked. Behind the criticism and inspiring it lay Denifle's conviction that Luther had wrought a terrible wrong to religion, and even to morality. The bitterness felt was expressed without reserve: he arraigned Luther as both a liar and a man of evil passions. It was painful reading. But its argument and its detailed criticism had to be faced.

In particular, Denifle dealt with Luther's picture of his early monastic[1] days and his spiritual experiences, a record of misery. We have pictures of these drawn in his later years. Denifle had little difficulty in showing that these were at variance with his letters of the early time itself, and with the maxims and teaching of authorities followed in monastic houses. Luther's later accounts were far more highly coloured than his early letters. Denifle scored an easy victory, and, as Figgis put it, he destroyed the "hagiographical" view of Luther.

Luther was much more of a popular preacher than a sound and well-read theologian. His theological education, somewhat scrappy, had been founded on the later Nominalists, especially Ockham and Gabriel Biel, for Erfurt was a "modernist" university. But in judging his character, apart from scholarship, his deep sense of the presence of God must not be forgotten, for of that presence, before which he stood as a sinful man, he was always deeply conscious. His sermons were popular pamphlets: a man who is able to "let himself go," gains a hold on the popular mind, but the very qualities which enable him to do this make it peculiarly difficult for him to trace with accuracy

---

[1] Technically Luther belonged to the reformed Saxon Congregation of Augustinian Friars, but, as they were organized and housed much like monks, we can speak of their monastic discipline.

his own growth, and to picture himself as he was years ago. The powers which go to strengthen his hold on an audience confuse him as he stands before his former self. There was, probably, in Luther's case, no wish to deceive, but accuracy was impossible, and confusion inevitable, for a man of his type.

The doctrinal position of Germany towards Luther's later years was settling down, even if into watchful camps it may be. His followers held Justification by Faith to be the one all-important article, and to be, in fact, the essence of the Reformation. It seemed to be such to Luther himself, and his disciples had come to believe that what he held then must be identical with what he had fought for in earlier years: Melanchthon, however, was passing into a different phase. He meditated much, as he said, on the doctrine of the Eucharist, and the bulk of the Lutherans grew to distrust him, and under Jesuit inspiration there were attempts to detach him. It was, as we have seen, a time of Conferences, such as that of Cassel (Dec. 1534), and of Articles, such as the Wittenberg Concord (May 1536). In this theological diplomacy, Bucer was the leading spirit: his great wish was to bring Zwinglians and Lutherans into accord on the Eucharist, where they differed most.

On the Catholic side, something of the same state was to come a little later. It was more or less assumed that the Tridentine position was identical with medieval doctrine. There were, it is true, some lines of cleavage among Catholic thinkers, but they were, for the most part, national rather than theological: Spanish ecclesiastics and French, for instance, had distinct tendencies of thought.

Most important, for wider, if not for merely personal, history, was Denifle's treatment of Luther's Lectures on the Epistle to the Romans, given at Wittenberg (April 1515 to October 1516). Denifle studied in the Vatican Library MS. notes on these Lectures made by Johann

Aurifaber:[1] the MS. had once belonged to the Library of Ulrich Fugger, had passed to the Palatinate Library at Heidelberg, and then been moved with the whole of that collection to the Vatican.

The Epistle to the Romans was, in itself, hard to interpret, and for the doctrinal interests of the Reformer was a specially fruitful field to cultivate. And the most important text was Romans i. 17. *Justitia enim Dei in eo revelatur ex fide in fidem*; *sicut scriptum est Justus autem ex fide vivat*. The history of the word "Justitia" reaches far, and at special periods is most significant. It was, for instance, the keynote of Hildebrand's life and reforms.[3] But *Justitia* (righteousness) had two meanings with medieval commentators. It might be the "active" sense: here the righteousness of God by which he punished sinners. Or it might be the "passive" sense, the righteousness which He imparted to sinners, so imputing his righteousness to them,

[1] Aurifaber was a boarder in Luther's home about 1540 onwards, and, like others whom he found there, took notes of the Master's talk, translating any Latin used into German: he did quite a little trade in Luther relics, and (1566) brought out an edition of the *Table Talk*, founded on his own notes and those of the other boarders, but these could hardly be depended upon for accuracy [See H. Böhmer, *Luther and the Reformation in the Light of Modern Research* (English trans. by E. S. G. Potter, London, 1930), pp. 177 *seq.*].

The MS. gives the *scholia* and the *glosses*. The glosses were short and written in the margin or interlined in the text: they are mere explanations of words and construction. The scholia are full explanations. The text used was the Vulgate: Luther's Hebrew was very elementary. But Luther, as a good lecturer, added much not in his notes.

[2] The details are given fairly in *Luther*, by Hartmann Grisar, S. J.: [English trans. by E. M. Lamond, London, 1913] vol. i. p. 630 and p. 184 *seq*. The MS. had been used by Dr. Vogel, but more thoroughly by Prof. J. Ficker [*Luther's Vorlesung über den Römerbrief*, Leipsig, 1908]. While he was editing it, Luther's own MS. of the Lectures was found in the State Library at Berlin, where it had been unnoticed since 1752: so Ficker was able to use it for his edition.

[3] I have tried to show this in my *Hildebrandine Essays* (Cambridge, 1932), especially pp. 33 and 80.

and regarding them as righteous. In the Preface to his Latin works (1545) Luther speaks of the misery he underwent by taking the word in the "active" sense. The same thing is spoken of in his *Table Talk*. All commentators, he said, gave this explanation, and so his horrors of mind and despair were intensified. But then suddenly, by what he held akin to a revelation, he saw that here it was the passive sense. And he described vividly the very time and place of this inspiration. Happiness came to him: he passed, as it were, through the very gates of Heaven itself. But this exegesis is held to be quite new: it was his and his alone.

But Denifle was able to give, what probably no other scholar could have done, a catena of passages from St. Augustine downwards to Luther's own day, proving that some seventy leading theologians had taken the passive sense.[1] And moreover he showed that Luther in his Lectures displayed a knowledge of this general interpretation. For instance in the works, which he used, of Peter Lombard and Nicholas of Lyra († 1340) this was the explanation given. So Luther's claim to a novel and original exegesis breaks down. He had learnt it from his guides, the ordinary books in common use. There is no doubt about the facts. Luther held his explanation of *Justitia* in the text of Romans to be quite new and original: in the course of years details were grouped around the all-important fact. And yet he had spoken in his lectures of authorities who had given this very explanation. A man may read a book, and thoughts or suggestions from it may remain with him. Years afterwards he may recall the idea but forget the book and its author: he may take it for a happy thought of his own. But this case was different. The use made of the authors, especially as said before, of Peter Lombard and Nicholas of Lyra, was enough to prevent a man taking the idea

---

[1] This was in the Quellenbelege to his *Luther und Luthertum* (vol. i., pt. ii.) [*Die abendländischen Schriftausleger bis Luther über "Iustitia Dei,"* Rom. i., 17 *und Iustificatio*].

for his own. It was no case of an idea resting in a fallow mind: a lecturer may happily forget much in his lectures, but forgetfulness, whole and complete, is hardly to be taken for granted here and in such a case.

And yet I think there is no doubt as to Luther's belief in what he said. It is quite true that in the case of the bigamy of Philip of Hesse, which some historians on both sides—Böhmer, for instance—discuss at such great length, Luther said they must lie boldly. That matter, so far as Philip and the second wife's mother were concerned, was morally disgraceful, and the Reformers, Luther and Melanchthon, were rightly discredited. But it seems to me that in the comment on this text in Romans, Luther really did believe what he was saying. How are we to explain it?

We have to find the explanation in Luther's mind. Luther had a vivid sense of his standing before God. Sin, which hid the face of God from him, was a dread reality to him. And with growing years, Justification by Faith became more and more of a cardinal doctrine with him. And the whole thing was rolled over and over again in his mind. I have known cases in which thoroughly honest men have suffered from what is called "defensive illusion," and have imagined something about themselves to be true and have spoken of it as real when it was purely imaginary. The self-justification becomes rooted in their mind, and they speak of it as actually true. I think that here we have such a case. I cannot, then, agree with the hostile critics who hold Luther here to be a deliberate liar. In just the same way with some elderly scholars, deeply concerned about some particular string of events, affecting themselves, the "defensive illusion" grows upon them. I have known more than one upright scholar who, in this way, have said, about some particular matter, and said more than once, what was not really true, but which, untrue as it was, he really believed, although the person to whom he spoke, by chance knew it to be untrue. And, for myself, I think that here with Luther we have such a case. We have this explanation, and while it does affect the particular question or incident, it does not affect the character of the man in other respects. Luther was a victim to such "a defensive illusion." A survey of Luther Literature, apart from any interest it may have, can teach us much. We see many personalities and characters interested and sharing in it: we see different phases of thought all bearing towards one centre. We see the by-paths and the pitfalls which await the stride of the historian. We see what is, perhaps, an unexpected comfort—how controversy attracts some who, in their later and better years, become sound and impartial historians: we see others who, unhappily, chose a more evil road, and become too controversial for history. The greatness of the literature, its persistence through so many phases, and the interest it carries from age to age are a symbol of the greatness, perhaps inexplicable of Luther himself.

After all, no man can be perfectly and properly understood, either in his personality or his action, until we know what he seemed to be in the eyes of his own generation and of those that came after. "No man liveth unto himself" : and this holds good not only for the short span of his life on earth, but for after ages as well. For the process of history is wide, and for the truth about any man and his doings, we have to pass beyond the narrow limit of his day. For most of us this may alter the estimate but little, and the impact of each upon history may be small. For others it may be great and last from age to age. This is the real test of greatness, and any character, judgments upon which stretch through the ages, is really great. Luther literature thus shows us Luther as really great.

ESSAY IV

LUTHERAN GERMANY AND THE EPISCOPATE

SYNOPSIS

LUTHERAN GERMANY AND THE EPISCOPATE

GERMANY, to many people, is a country which stands peculiarly for the Reformation. Here the ordinary abuses were felt as they were elsewhere. From the middle of the fifteenth century up to the Council of Trent complaints, embodied in the so-called *Centum Gravamina*,[1] had presented German grievances. Strictly speaking, the ordinary evils of clerical life at the time, which should have been dealt with by efficient Episcopal control, formed part of the complaint; others concerned the relations between the Curia and Germany. The comparative freedom of France and England, secured by Concordats, had thrown the burden of Papal headship, and especially its taxation, mainly upon Germany; hence arose not only great discontent, but also a great dislocation of ecclesiastical machinery.

And there were other evils peculiar to Germany. Nowhere were Chapters more corrupt and evil: nowhere were they regarded so openly as provisions for younger sons of nobles.[2] Hence instead of being centres of spiritual life, cathedrals were too often sources of evil. Bishoprics were treated in the same way, only they were kept in the princely families. Pluralities were common: Consecration or even

---

[1] In Brown's *Fasciculus*, i. 352. See *Cambridge Modern History*, i. 690.

[2] See Stubbs, *Lectures on European History*, p. 63, on the deeply-rooted evils; the ecclesiastical states were well governed, but "religiously regarded the system has hardly a redeeming feature." Ph. Schneider, *Die bischöflichen Domkapital*: (Mayence, 1885), an excellent account of the institutions. At Augsburg sons of citizens were ineligible for canonries and their exclusion became very strict. See *Die Augsburger Domkapital im Mittelalter*: Otto Leuze (Augsburg, 1908), pp. 4–5.

Ordination was long postponed by elected Bishops. Consequently, as a working power the Episcopate was in many parts almost useless: it was generally without spiritual intention. When at length a revival came, beginning early in the sixteenth century, it scarcely affected the North. Thus it may be said that the Episcopate was more closely connected with the princely families than with the national life, and that it worked as they did, more for disunion than for union.

In two other countries much affected by Calvinism, the Episcopate had not grown with the nation's growth. In Switzerland, where the growth of the nation had been almost accidental, ecclesiastical unity was weak; the five Swiss dioceses were divided between three provinces, with centres in other lands. In the Netherlands things were much the same; the dioceses were mixed with foreign territory, and the Archbishops over them were also foreign.[1] There was no religious coherence, no sufficient provision for control. Charles V, who wished to give a coherent ecclesititical unity to the country, and Philip II proposed to supply these defects, and the proposal, for various reasons, became one cause of the great Revolt.[2]

These special blemishes are to be found in countries which showed the greatest dislike to Church order and the ancient system, in countries where Episcopacy was afterwards most completely thrown aside. Was such a result to be wondered at? Was it likely that a Church, weakly organised, weighed down alike by the greatness of its duties

---

[1] In Switzerland, Constance and Chur (Coire) were under Mayence; Basle and Lausanne under Besançon: Sitten (Sion) under Tarantaise until exempted by Leo X.

[2] See Armstrong's *Charles V*, ii. 336 f., *Cambridge Modern History*, iii. 186. Also Pastor, vi. (German edn.), pp. 550–52, and Kidd, *Documents of the Continental Reformation*, p. 684, where a letter from the Venetian ambassador illustrates the need for an increase of Bishops and the difficulty of providing it owing to existing Papal and Episcopal interests.

and by a feeling of its unfitness, could cope with a crisis or face a flood? To say this is not to make an apology, but to state a fact. There will always arise, from time to time, great movements full of force, for good if properly directed, for evil if left uncontrolled. To control them, to utilise them for the work of Christ, is the Church's task. To consider the opportunities for doing this, to devise machinery for it, is the special task of Bishops, the leaders of the Church. And it is here that the Episcopate, sometimes from its defective organisation, sometimes from its personal weakness, has so often failed; here, on the other hand, it has often triumphed gloriously, and saved the world. It has brought to the possible licence of the present the restraining power of the past. Here is the test, then, which we instinctively apply to it and to its individual members. We call them great when they rise to this their special powers:

> Souls temper'd with fire,
> Fervent, heroic and good,
> Helpers and friends of mankind,
>
> . . . . .
>
> Strengthen the wavering line,
> Stablish, continue our march
> On, to the City of God.
>
> (*Rugby Chapel.*)

It is then, I think, not an accident that the disruptive force of the Reformation was greatest where the Episcopate was most corrupt or inefficient and least connected with the national life. We may note the words of Dr. Stubbs who wrote:[1] "I hope you will not ascribe it to mere professional zeal, if I say that one of the great openings for the Reformation was made by the absence in some countries of Europe of adequate episcopal superintendence. It may have been quite one of the subordinate causes, but you will find it the rule: where the dioceses are large and the bishops few and powerful, there their temptation to secular business

[1] See Lectures on *Modern European History*, p. 33 f.

is the greater, the machinery of the Church is found to be loose and ill-adjusted, religion lifeless; and consequently, whether you regard the Reformation as a good or as an evil, the way for renunciation of the dominant religion is opened." He then goes on to speak of the confused ecclesiastical organisation of the Netherlands; there as in Switzerland the bond of national life might have been made stronger by a coherent ecclesiastical unity.

Both the Zwinglian movement and Calvinism were ecclesiastically more revolutionary than was Lutheranism. The Reformation at Zürich,[1] indeed, took a special form, a revolt of a town against its Bishop who lived in a neighbouring city, Constance. On the negative side this was, as Ranke pointed out long ago, its special characteristic, while other features were due to its working in a democratic city-state. At Geneva, too, religious change was complicated by struggles against the Bishop; the renunciation of his authority was the beginning of the Reformation. Luther again, friar as he was, with a monastic training, had no special regard for an episcopal authority and guidance to which, indeed, he owed but little. Yet he was not revolutionary from mere wantonness, and it is possible that had the Episcopate presented itself to him in a worthier moral and spiritual guise, the story of the German Reformation might have been other than it was. Had there been in the Church a moral leadership such as he found in Staupitz, whom he followed so well; had there been in it a coherent organisation such as that of the State, to which he kept so closely, his outlook might have been far other than it was.

The Augsburg Confession speaks of Bishops in a guarded and moderate tone.[2] After stating that the ecclesiastical

---

[1] See *Cambridge Modern History*, ii. ch. x.

[2] The document itself in Kidd, *Documents of the Continental Reformation*, p. 259, and in Schaff, *The Creeds of the Evangelical Protestant Churches*, p. 3, pt. i. art. 22. "Concerning ecclesiastical government they teach that no man should publicly in the Church

power, and the power of the sword, have been inconveniently confused, it goes on: "Now our judgment is this: that the

---

teach or administer the Sacraments, except he be rightly called." Pt. ii. art. 7, "There have been great controversies touching the power of Bishops; in which many have inconveniently mixed together ecclesiastical power and the power of the sword. . . . Now their judgment (i.e. *that of godly and learned men*) is this, that the power of the keys, or the power of Bishops, according to the Gospel, is a power or command of God of preaching the Gospel, of remitting or retaining sins and of administering the Sacraments. For Christ sends His apostles with this command, etc. . . . If so be that the Bishops have any power of the sword, this they have not as Bishops by the command of the Gospel but by man's law given by kings and emperors for the civil administration of their goods. . . . When, therefore, it is inquired of concerning the jurisdiction of Bishops, government (*imperium*) must be distinguished from ecclesiastical jurisdiction. Further, according to the Gospel, or as they say of divine right, no jurisdiction belongs (*competit*) to Bishops as Bishops, that is, as those to whom is committed the ministry of the Word and Sacraments, save to remit sins, also to discern doctrine, and to reject doctrine discordant from the Gospel and to shut out from the communion of the Church ungodly men whose impiety is known, without human force but by the Word. And herein of necessity and by divine right the Churches ought to render them obedience according to that (saying), 'He who heareth you heareth Me.'

"But when they teach or determine anything against the Gospel then the Churches have a command from God which forbids obedience," etc. (Matt. vii. 15; Gal. i. 8, etc., *and quoting St. Augustine*).

"Besides these things there is a question whether Bishops or Pastors have the authority to institute ceremonies in the Church, and to lay down laws anent foods and holidays, degrees or orders of ministers, etc. Those who ascribe this power to the Bishops allege the testimony, *I have yet*, etc. (John xvi. 12, 13). They allege also . . . (Acts xv. 29). They allege the change of the Sabbath into the Lord's Day against the Decalogue as it seems. They assert the power of the Church to be great because it has dispensed from a precept of the Decalogue."

"But of this question one side teaches this: that the Bishops have not the power of determining anything against the Gospel, as was shown above; the same thing do teach the Canons, *Dist.* 9, etc."

"It remaineth, therefore, since ordinances instituted as necessary or with the opinion of meriting grace are repugnant to the Gospel, that it is lawful for any Bishops to institute or demand such laws.

power of the keys, or the power of the Bishops, by the rule
of the Gospel is a power or commandment from God
of preaching the Gospel, of remitting and retaining sins,
and of administering the Sacraments. But if Bishops have
any power of the sword, they have it, not as Bishops,
by command of the Gospels, but as a gift from human
law." It is true the Confession goes on further to say
(in words reminding us of Wiclif's doctrine of "dominion
founded on grace") that when Bishops order anything contrary to the Gospel, Christians have a command to disobey
them. It also places this same limit upon the right claimed
for Bishops of instituting ceremonies. But after all these
considerations, the upshot is that "The Bishops might easily
retain lawful obedience if they would not press the keeping
of traditions which cannot be kept with good conscience.
Our endeavour is not that the domination of Bishops should
be removed, but we seek the one thing that they would
suffer the Gospel to be taught purely, and relax some few
observances which cannot be kept without sin." Here there
is, of course, that appeal to individual conscience, as opposed
to Church authority, which played so vital a part at the
Reformation. There are also many criticisms which might
be made upon the language and the special expressions
used. But the paradox was true then as it is now: the in-

For it is necessary that the doctrine concerning Christian liberty be
maintained in the Churches, etc." [*Matters coming under these heads
are discussed at length.*]

"The Bishops might easily retain lawful obedience, if they would not
urge men to keep such traditions as are not able to be kept with a good
conscience."

"Peter (1 Pet. v. 3) forbids Bishops to lord it and to give command
to the Churches. Now it is not urged (*non id agitur*) that rule should
be taken from the Bishops, but that this one thing should be demanded:
that they suffer the Gospel to be taught purely, and relax a certain
few observances which cannot be kept without sin. But if they will
remit none, let them see in what way they will give account to God
in that by their pertinacity they give cause of schism." The English
translation here given is, with some verbal changes, that of Schaff.

dividual conscience at its best and the Church's command at its best should never be opposed and it is an evil thing when they seem to conflict. Were the Church within its rights, and were the individual conscience well instructed, conflict could not well arise. But after all these drawbacks are made, the Confession does not take up a hostile attitude towards the Episcopate, as some later Confessions did.

Luther's view in his *Address to the Nobility* is guarded, especially for such a vehement writer. He says: "It should be decreed by an imperial law, that no episcopal pallium, and no confirmation of any appointment shall for the future be obtained from Rome. The order of the most holy and renowned Nicene Council must again be restored, namely that a Bishop must be confirmed by the two nearest Bishops, or by the Archbishops. If the Pope cancels the decrees of these and all other councils, what is the good of councils at all? Who has given him the right thus to despise councils and to cancel them? If this is allowed, we had better abolish all Bishops, Archbishops and Primates, and make simple rectors of them all, so that they would have the Pope alone over them; as is indeed the case now; he deprives Bishops, Archbishops and Primates of all the authority of their office, taking everything to himself, and leaving them only the name and the empty title; more than this, by his exemption he has withdrawn convents, abbots and prelates from the ordinary authority of the Bishops, so that there remains no order in Christendom. The necessary result of this must be, and has been, laxity in punishing, and such a liberty to do evil in all the world, that I very much fear one might call the Pope 'the man of sin.' Who but the Pope is to blame for this absence of all order, of all punishment, of all government, of all discipline in Christendom? By his own arbitrary power he ties the hands of all his prelates, and takes from them their rods, while all their subjects have their hands unloosed, and obtain licence by gift or purchase." He goes on to suggest that on matters which cannot be settled by the local Bishops and Archbishops, there should be an appeal to the Pope, while a national Consistory for Germany should exercise jurisdiction, giving their due weight to the temporal authorities. To sum up he hopes so "to help the German nation to become a free people of Christians."[1] Some of his language is more violent than was needed for his proposals, but caution marks the standpoint of his *Primary Works* (Aug. 1520). As justification for this picture of deeply rooted evils Luther could have quoted many who were never on his side, and one of the most learned of later Germans, Döllinger, puts the matter much in the same way. "And the German Church? Where was it then, and how did it help itself? The Germans had still indeed a political unity: the Empire, with the Emperor and the Imperial Diet; and they had Bishops and dioceses. But there was wanting a higher organisation of common life: in a word, a German national Church. For centuries no German council had been held, nor anything done to remedy even the grossest and most crying abuses. In truth, such a Council was hardly possible, and it is a significant fact that during the whole forty years of the Reformation contest, neither the German Episcopate nor even any considerable portion of it, made a single attempt to take counsel in Synod on the religious situation and the common measures to be adopted. There is scarcely a parallel case in all Church history, but it is explained by their conscious impotence. For since the dismemberment of the entire Church system through the Popes, the German Church lay on the ground like a helpless and motionless giant with fettered limbs."[2]

[1] *To the Christian Nobility of the German Nation respecting the reformation of the Christian Estate*, iii. 3 f. I quote the translation in Wace and Buchheim: *Luther's Primary Works*, p. 45 f. (with the verbal correction of pallium for cloak).

[2] Döllinger, *Lectures on the Reunion of the Churches*, delivered in 1872, translated by Oxenham, pp. 68–9. Bp. Hall (*Episcopacy by Divine Right, Introduction, Sect. III*) is excellent on the Lutheran

It is true that Luther was not always consistent, and in his scheme of organisation he discarded Bishops. But he regarded his Visitors as substitutes for them. In his preface to Melanchthon's Instructions for them he said: "Now, since by Divine mercy the light of the Gospel is restored, and that disgraceful confusion of the Christian Church is stayed, we have wished indeed to bring back that true office of Bishops and Visitation: but since no one of us was called or ordered to undertake so great a work we have humbly sought from the Serene Elector John," to undertake the work and send fit men to discharge it[1] (1527); and in the preface to his Short Catechism[2] he spoke of the neglect on the part of the Bishops in discharging the duty for which they had been appointed. But on the other hand in fairness we should bear in mind the changes and disorders for which Luther himself was largely responsible ("There is no fear of God, no more discipline since the papal ban has gone, and every one does what he lists," is the way he himself puts it in his letter to the Elector), although the covetousness of the rulers had helped. But the upshot is that the Lutheran movement was not a reaction against a good episcopal system soundly worked. It began when that system, through causes we have already noted, was weak and ineffective. There were, moreover, in Germany those who, like Colet in England, pleaded for the restoration of full episcopal authority as a better way than revolution. Melanchthon, who was widely criticised in his day as afterwards for his so-called weakness, which was often only moderation, understood the meaning of the Episcopate, and felt its loss much more than did Luther.

---

attitude towards Episcopacy. He hoped (1639) for their adoption of it. So did most Anglicans.

[1] Extracts from the Preface and Instructions in Kidd's *Documents*, p. 202 f. See also McGiffert's *Martin Luther*, pp. 311–312.

[2] See Kidd, p. 206 f. Extracts are given from the letter to the elector in Vetter, p. 276. The date is November 22, 1526.

But Luther himself was, sometimes at any rate, prepared to admit Bishops as restraints, and to his friend and colleague Arnsdorf he spoke significantly of his visitors as being "all Bishops." But the use of the expression was in itself a testimony to that disregard of the Church's traditions and past which was one of his great characteristics.

When we turn to Melanchthon, who was in many ways a conservative force, we find he would have liked to see something like episcopal rule. In the cities the civil power of the Bishops had brought upon them enmity and dislike: the magnificence and civil importance of the German Prince-Bishops had been bought at a heavy cost to the Church. Melanchthon noted, too, the wish of the cities for freedom from episcopal lordship; to them, in Germany as in Switzerland, it was more a matter of civil than ecclesiastical liberty.[1] But to him, owing to his primary concern with doctrine, there was an obstacle to the preservation of the old Bishops in their dislike of the new doctrine; he would have preferred, therefore, had he been able to act freely, to bring in Bishops of a new type; to put it in other words, he saw the advantages which belonged to episcopal administration. When after the Counter-Reformation an efficient Episcopate was at length revived in his country it brought with it theological ideas very different from those he had (perhaps somewhat reluctantly) adopted. His views, like his career, illustrate the fears, the dangers and the losses that attended a non-episcopal reformation

All these varying views which lay beneath the surface of the German Reformation had their counterpart in its history, in the earlier stage in the organisation and in later stages in the controversies. In Brandenburg and Prussia,

[1] For Nuremberg, which was in the diocese of the Bishop of Bamberg, favourably disposed as he was to Lutheranism, see Ranke's *Reformation in Germany and Switzerland* (Routledge's edn., 1905), p. 470 f. For Saxon Visitation, Ranke, 465.

where the Bishops themselves had turned towards reform, there were for a time attempts to preserve the succession as there were in other places, and to secure something of the old control.[1]

Two characteristics of German Lutheranism, its dependence upon Princes in matters of administration, and its absorbing interest in theological controversy, are seen outside the German Empire also. The Scandinavian kingdoms both in ecclesiastical changes[2] and political interests had been drawn into the Germanic system. They were affected by the Reformation, and also by the mixed conditions of the seventeenth century in Germany, a period which has been well described by Döllinger.[3] "The whole church system remained in the hands of Consistories under royal control. And to this must be added the theological ossification and narrow rigidity of the doctrines which had to be maintained according to the Formula of Concord. From these causes sprang a twofold reaction among the laity and the theologians. The lay reaction manifested itself partly in the growing frequency of conversions to Catholicism; many felt the authority of Popes and Councils to be preferable to that of a secular prince. On the other hand, the whole religious literature of the laity, from the seventeenth to far into the eighteenth century, is penetrated by a profound dissatisfaction with the condition of the system and prevalent teaching of the Protestant Church." In this direction the influence of the "mediating" theo-

---

[1] For the documents about these lands, see Kidd, p. 318.

[2] Lord Acton says (*History of Freedom and other Essays*, p. 341), "The theological literature of Sweden consists almost entirely of translations from the German." He also says (p. 340), "The Danish Church has given no sign of life, and has shown no desire for independence since the Reformation." But this did not prevent great zeal for Missions. Years later he told me he thought Nielsen's *History of the Papacy*, written by a Danish Bishop, the best in existence.

[3] Döllinger, *Lectures on the Reunion of the Churches*, p. 85 f. (Eng. trans. by H. N. Oxenham, London, 1872).

logians[1] should be remembered. To them, as afterwards to Grotius in the Protestant camp, an appeal to the primitive Church was the only possible road to union as well as the only security for reform. But matters had now gone too far for such an appeal to have much effect: it might move individuals to a change of creed, but, on the Continent at any rate, it could not bring religious bodies any nearer unity between themselves. At Ratisbon (1541) an agreement between Catholics and Protestants might have been reached upon doctrines such as Justification, although Rome was less disposed for concord here and on this matter than was Germany. But there was less chance of agreement on practical matters, on the liability to error of General Councils, and on the primacy of the Pope. Sacramental teaching was another obstacle. But after all it was political considerations all round; the position of the Papacy on the one side, and the independent interests of the new theologians on the other, which were the great obstacles to union. And afterwards the two parties diverged still more: the Catholics hardened in their Papalism, and the Protestants in their rigidity of Lutheran doctrine. But for a time it had seemed as if the appeal to the primitive Church, involving, as that appeal did, the succession of Bishops with the rights of ordination and government, might have provided ground for union. It is instructive to compare the position in Germany with that in England. For when we do this, and only when we do it, can we understand the exact force of the appeal to primitive times. That appeal was not, as so many people assume, merely an argument. It lay at the very root of the Church's life, with its continued tradition, and the neglect of it, by the one side in order to keep up the Papacy, by the other side to enforce Lutheran doctrine, led in Germany to untold evils and multiplied

[1] Döllinger, *Reunion*, p. 77 f. Pastor in vol. v. p. 294 f. (German edn.), especially about the Colloquy of Regensburg, gives a full account. For documents, see Kidd, p. 341 f.

divisions. It was the good fortune of the English Church, by its history and through its leaders to keep the Episcopate with its possibilities of union. To do so it had to reject the Papal leadership on one hand, and to reject the doctrines and the model of the "best reformed Churches" on the other hand. But in the Episcopate it found a real basis for unity as we can see in the reign of Elizabeth with its comparative although not entire success. The English Church stood as a witness for Episcopacy in a unique way, and the importance of that witness is illustrated though in an opposite way by the course of events in Germany.

Some German theologians, especially after Calvinistic influence had become powerful, were strengthened in their resistance to Episcopacy by the inferences from the supposed identity of Bishops and Presbyters or Priests in the New Testament.[1] But to found Church organisation upon this assumption or supposed result of criticism was to cast away the whole history of the past and to make a breach which was more than a mechanical interruption in continuous life. Much discussion has been given to the definition of the Church just as to that of a nation, and a comparison of the two conceptions is instructive. A nation has been confused with a nationality, which is an entity of race; it has also been confused with a State, which is an entity of law. These two conceptions, Nationality and State, belong respectively to ethnology and jurisprudence. But the discussion of nations belongs to history, and it is history which alone can define a nation. It is a body of people made one by their history; and it is history alone which can determine whether any given body of people is truly a nation or not. In the same way it is the province of ecclesiastical history to deal with Churches. Some would make a Church depend solely upon purity of doctrine: others would make it depend solely upon its organisation at any given time. They would

---

[1] It should not be forgotten that Hort and Harnack are two formidable dissenters from this view of identity.

make the definition a matter of theology or of ecclesiastical order. But the real test is a community of history which links together the people concerned, and links them also with the past paying due regard to both Doctrine and Order. This shuts out any haphazard association or deliberate formation, for neither of these can make a Church. And it also demands continuity between the special body under consideration and the primitive Church. In that unity, where it is found to exist, purity of doctrine and continuity of organisation necessarily play a part. But it is history which alone can determine what is and what is not a part of the Church. Revolutions which overthrow organisation or interfere with doctrine may or may not be of such a kind as to destroy the unity of history. But the force and limits of revolution are not capable of exact human calculation, and it is not to be lightly undertaken just because the fear of such a disaster seems small.

I do not pretend that this definition makes the consideration easier. But anybody who has watched discussions which turn upon the definition of the Church cannot have failed to notice the difficulties that have often arisen. The supposed test has been of clear application, but in the end the judgment has not been easy to give. The test of organisation has been applied, and then it has seemed necessary to bring in some further considerations based upon doctrine to modify or to affect the conclusion. Or it may have been the other way round: the test of doctrine has been applied, and the verdict reached upon it may have seemed unsatisfactory: to modify or to change it supplementary considerations about organisation have been brought in, so that the original discussion has been enlarged. To me it seems that such confusion, such an unsatisfactory result of much labour and discussion, is inevitable when the argument has been started upon a mistaken or an incomplete definition; it is a mental process we often see. When we have to decide whether any part of Christendom has kept its corporate membership in the Catholic Church or not, we have to look at the whole of its history instead of looking only at some special date or particular characteristic.

Nowhere is this consideration more difficult and this caution more needed than in the case of the Scandinavian lands. To begin with, Christian Europe had only fitfully felt its responsibility for them in days when they were heathen, and the organisation of the Church was never made effective there.[1] But in Norway and Denmark the respect formerly shown towards the Bishops lived on, even in the stress of the Reformation and under German influence, in the regard shown towards the Superintendents who replaced them. In Sweden there were also efforts to keep the succession, and the drifting away from the old Church system was gradual and sometimes hardly conscious. In its later history Lutheranism generally has shown, more especially at times, a sense of loss in respect of the Episcopate,[2] just as it has in respect to liturgic services. Thus, for instance, Frederick I, first King of Prussia, appointed two

[1] For the history, see some details in Willson's *History of Church and State in Norway*. The documents, with useful references, in Kidd, *Documents*, p. 131 *seq.*, p. 233 *seq.*, and p. 322 *seq.*; see also the late Bishop of Salisbury's *History of the Church in Sweden*. See the *Encyclical Letter of the Lambeth Conference*, 1908, p. 181.

[2] For further details see Döllinger, *Reunion*, p. 88 f. Ranke, *Memoirs of the House of Brandenburg* and *History of Prussia during the Seventeenth and Eighteenth Centuries*, i. 107 f. and 463 f. Abbey and Overton, *The English Church in the Eighteenth Century*, p. 160 f. Lathbury, *The History of the Book of Common Prayer* (a work which, like the same author's *History of Convocation*, is full of sound learning, with details often neglected by other writers), p. 430 f. See also for the references (in Krüger's *Handbuch der Kirchengeschichte*), vol. iii., Hermelink, *Reformation und Gegenreformation*, § 60–2, vol. iv. Stephen, *Die Neuzeit*, § 4 : 5, § 11 : 6, § 45:1 5. On the Union (which began in 1817) see § 45 : 4. Also Acton, *The History of Freedom and other Essays*, p. 345. There is much in the same Essay, a review of Döllinger's *Kirche und Kirchen*, on the history of Doctrine in the Lutheran bodies. The conservative standpoint was taken by Stahl and is illustrated in his important work *Der Lutheranische Kirche und*

Bishops, one for the Lutherans, and one for the Reformed[1] who were to dignify his coronation. Then there followed attempts not only at reunion between the two bodies of Lutheran and Reformed (or Calvinistic), but also to use for its accomplishment the example and influence of the English Church. The Book of Common Prayer drew to itself admiration then as it had done for instance long before, from French Catholics in the days of Elizabeth.[2] Jablonski, a Pole and chaplain to Frederick I of Prussia, had become a warm advocate of the Anglican system, and along with others had the English Liturgy translated with a view to use in the royal Chapel (1706).

Those in England who were interested in the matter understood that in many places there was a willingness to admit of Episcopacy and plans for its introduction were actually prepared.[3] The movement towards unity and restoration had behind it not only local sympathy, but international feeling. Bossuet, whose position in France answered in some ways to that of Leibnitz in Germany,

---

die Union, Berlin, 1860. Lord Acton in conversation with Döllinger (*Hist. Freedom*, p. 391) mentioned Stahl, speaking of him as "the greatest man born of a Jewish mother since Titus." Döllinger thought this unjust to Disraeli. But he thought Stahl "the most illustrious lay champion" of the Lutheran party.

[1] At the coronation Frederick crowned himself and his Queen and was then anointed by the Bishops. See *Cambridge Modern History*, v. 665. "Few coronations so frankly unspiritual" are recorded, says Sir A. W. Ward. Döllinger (*Reunion*, p. 82) says these "bishops" received English consecration. The Rev. Prof. C. Jenkins told me that there is no trace of this at Lambeth, and the *Life of Archbishop Sharp* (York), i. 403 f., disproves the statement.

[2] Throgmorton wrote from France to Burleigh that the formulary of the Church of England was less repugnant to the Papists than the continental Protestant forms, and Walsingham confirmed this view later.

[3] Abbey and Overton (small edn.), p. 162. On some points in later liturgic history of the Lutherans, see Stephan (Krüger's *Handbuch* as before, iv.), pp. 76 f. and 232.

was concerned in the movement, while the part played by Leibnitz himself in it helped to bring upon him the reproach of being a Papist at heart. Politics, however, were mingled in the negotiations, and after weighing heavily among the considerations that furthered them, proved in the end disastrous to them. These political interests, and the change from a tolerance founded on learning to philosophic indifference proved too much to overcome. A century which began with the enlightened piety of Leibnitz ended in the destructive trifling of Voltaire. This catastrophe was as great in its way as was the apparent disappearance of the mediating theologians two centuries before. Leibnitz held that "the Protestants ought to accept any doctrine proved to have been universally received in the ancient Church of the Roman Empire."[1] His correspondence with Bossuet should not be forgotten. Others of very different views had reached the same conclusion in themselves, and among them was the Jesuit, Moritz Volta, Confessor to the King of Poland. He was a frequent visitor to the Prussian Court under Frederick I, and "one of his favourite ideas was, that a reunion of the Church might take place on the ground of the doctrines of the Fathers and of the early Councils."[2] Had the authoritative tradition of the primitive Church been accepted in the West as it was in the East, the sense of unity might have proved a check against the twofold revolution which deepened discord. But the exaltation of the Papacy, so thoroughly carried out at Trent, combined with its apparent enemy, Protestant individualism, to hinder this result. Thus an end was put to a process which might have repaired the breach made by the Reformation. It is, therefore, not alto-

[1] Döllinger, *Reunion*, p. 94. *The Reunion of the Churches, a Study of G. W. Leibnitz and his Great Attempt*, G. J. Jordan (London, 1927), has much of interest. For foreign books, see *Cambridge Mod. Hist.*, vol. v., ch. iv. and xxi., Bibliographies.

[2] Ranke, *Prussia*, i. 117–18.

gether fair to blame the energy and the destructiveness of the Reformers for all that happened after them. It is true that the conception held by some of the Church's history as a mere process of corruption must often have deprived them of power and hope. But this disadvantage they often managed to evade. Great movements have nearly always some elements in them which, if allowed their freedom, grow strong enough to counteract the possible excesses. It was so with the Reformation. The strangling of these elements was the work of the seventeenth century, and caused many of the evils we often ascribe to the Reformation period itself. The organisation of the Church as it grows from age to age is capable of meeting the evils these ages bring. Outside pressure and forces such as that of the State only interfere with the working of that constitution or check its growth. It is this free action of the Church itself which is implied in the phrase "the Historic Episcopate," and it has been well said that "the abandonment of the Episcopate was not a natural result of the Reformation. It was not a part of the Lutheran movement."[1] The process we have just considered warns us against neglecting the past history of the Church or departing from its working constitution. It is an instructive chapter of history.

One cause of this misfortune is to be found in the action of the German sovereigns, and especially of the House of Brandenburg. Christian Thomasius (†1728),[2] a theologian

---

[1] By the late Prof. C. A. Briggs in his *Church Unity*, p. 95.

[2] On Thomasius, one of the earliest Germans to protest against the use of torture and trials for witchcraft, see Alzog, *Universal Church History* (translated by Byrne, Dublin, 1900), iv. 81–3; and Schlosser, *History of the Eighteenth Century*, i. 183 f. He is one of the leading figures in the University history of his day; amid colleagues described as being as rough as were the students, he spread an enthusiasm for knowledge; he was one of the first to lecture in German instead of Latin, and to popularise knowledge started a magazine with an attractive title in thirteen long words, which after a year was changed to a still more attractive title in eighteen longer words. The periodical lasted three years. Thomasius belonged to a time when German

of widespread influence, and one of the founders of the University of Halle (1694), had taught the duty of the ruler to suppress all controversy and Frederick William I (1713–40), in his more than fatherly care for Prussia, newly made a kingdom (1701), became an apt pupil of this school. The Consistory, which regulated ecclesiastical matters, represented the King "in his character of supreme Bishop."[1] The religious unity[2] which was demanded in the interest of the State became, under the pressure of the monarchy, a suppression of differences; all convictions were to be held equally true, and all sincere believers within the limits of Lutheranism and Calvinism were to form one religious body. This system was much like the "toleration" of the Long Parliament and its successors which also had their own impassable limits of Popery and Prelacy, or again much like modern undenominationalism, which, in its search for unity, loses all vitality. All of them, too, had much the same promise of success, and the same disappointment in disastrous results. The Prussian conception, thus brought into practical politics by Frederick William I,[3]

Lutheranism was a living religious and moral power, not a mere worship of the State. Francis Hutchinson (more or less Arian), Prof. of Moral Science at Glasgow, 1729–1747, was the first to lecture there in English (Lecky, *England*, ii. 538).

[1] Ranke, *Prussia*, I. 463–4.

[2] See previous note, p. 82: also as before Stephan (*Neuzeit*), IV. 24 and 79, for earlier attempts; for the Union, *ibid.*, pp. 227–9. See also Acton, *History of Freedom and other Essays*, p. 345. "In 1817 the Prussion Union added a new Church to the two original forms of Protestantism."

[3] On this monarch's religious policy, see *Cambridge Modern History*, vi. 226. ("Of course in a State so rigorously absolutist . . . there could be no question of liberty for the Church.") I do not think most English students would accept the contrast drawn by the writer, Dr. Emil Daniel, between the Prussian Protestanism with its "vivifying spirit" and the "apathy" of the English Church. But of the Prussian absolutism there is no doubt and the English Church somewhat disregarded its own system.

culminated a century later in the Union, brought forward by Frederick William III, and discussed under Frederick William IV; great turmoil was aroused by its appearance. It was to have been the end of strife, but instead led to a fresh controversy; its working joined to the pressure of the State's heavy hand[1] checked religious zeal and spiritual growth. Nevertheless, all aspirations after the episcopal succession did not disappear. Under Frederick William IV the ill-starred scheme of the Jerusalem bishopric, so well known in the beginning of the Oxford movement, was meant, so far as it affected Germany, to be the small beginning of a Prussian Episcopate. But nothing came of it in this direction; the forces hostile to a free episcopal system and all that it brings with it seemed to gather strength, and everything was swallowed up in the extension of a highly centralised state. Not even the influence of the Pietists and of the Moravian Brethren which blossomed out into many missionary enterprises and deepened spiritual religion among individuals could arrest the progress of corporate decay.

To sum up, then, what we have seen. Out of the midst of darkness there came an effort at reform which was both persistent and in the end effective. It was destined to appear, although in different shapes, at the Council of Trent and in England. In Spain the influence of the movement was especially strong, and through it the National Church was reorganised and revived. The Spanish Bishops, a compact and noble band, at Trent were firm supporters of Episcopacy in its earlier form before the Papacy had seized its powers. But in some countries Church organisation was weak both in itself and in its hold upon national life. There, and there above all, the forces of disruption gained strength: the surroundings favoured their growth: there was no power able to stay them. It is thus that the

[1] On the question of Church and State among Lutherans and in Prussia, see Acton, *History of Freedom*, p. 319 f.

sins of the Church bear their ghastly fruit, and the evils that generations do live after them.

But already in our review of the history we have seen an unexpected force and power in the Episcopate as an institution: it is not a mere restraint for lawlessness and disorder, as some Lutherans held and some modern critics seem to suppose: it is not an engine of government which can be brought into close connexion with the spiritualities and emotions, the practice and the usage of religion. It is not something to be imposed from without, or to be copied from outside. It has a mysterious strength and a many-sided energy of its own, with a power of growth and of adaptation from age to age. In its earliest days it arose from the innermost life of Christ's Church, and it spread with inexplicable speed and success.[1] So too in later ages it was entwined with all that was best and most fruitful of the Church's ministry: it absorbed its spirituality and it moulded its practice. Where it was missing, or when it was lacking in its ideal or its work, evils arose and grew rampant and the best men longed for reform. Its absence or its weakness brought a sense of wrong. It seemed to be in itself Christianity in the form that could best guide nations, whether early converts or ripened Christians, on their road towards God. It was more of an inspiration than a conception or an expedient. Men might well regard it as a mysterious working of the living power of Christ, one of the necessary activities of His body on earth. Even where its action had been retarded by the pressure of politics or the sloth of mankind, it had yet done much of its work, and given perpetual promise of a revived ideal and a richer life.

As we turn the pages of the past, and read there long sequences of cause and effect, our sense of responsibility is quickened, and the promise of our hopes enlarged;

[1] See Sermon IV., *The Place of the Episcopate in Christian History:* Dean Church in the volume Pascal and other Sermons (London, 1895).

we see the power of human error, but we also see behind it the grandeur of human effort. The corporate life can never excuse the individual sloth, but, in the corporate life, the individual labour finds its consecrated end. For it is so that we see the building fitly framed together, growing into a holy temple for the Lord: it is so we feel ourselves builded together "for a habitation of God through the Spirit."

ESSAY V

THE GROWTH OF PAPAL JURISDICTION BEFORE NICHOLAS I

K

SYNOPSIS

SYNOPSIS

131

THE GROWTH OF PAPAL JURISDICTION
BEFORE NICHOLAS I

THE papacy of Leo the Great gives us a good halting place in papal history; it closes one period and leaves another to begin. The Bishop of Imperial Rome could never be a mere ecclesiastical official of the greatest city; while it had been the home of Emperors he had been often enough a trusted adviser to them; when it ceased to be their dwelling-place fresh responsibilities and new opportunities came to him. There is hardly need even to mention the change due to the foundation of a new Rome in the East, with its fresh magnificence, so largely brought from the Western capital, and with its political outlook on the richest and most important provinces. Moreover the wealth of the Roman Church had long been great and it was matched by its Christian generosity; its influence in this way had passed into a tradition, which grew steadily from the time of St. Ignatius onward. In all the cities where a church had been founded there was Christian organisation, and the Roman episcopate could not but profit by the business-like methods of the imperial and civic governments. Roman ecclesiastics were naturally distinguished for the same characteristics as were the civilians. The *gravitas Romana* could be noted even in the eleventh century, and its mere existence would have given peculiar weight to the decisions of Roman Bishops and the decrees of Roman councils. Everywhere throughout the provinces local churches and local municipalities had almost alone stood the shock of the barbarian hordes; these inheritances from the past were naturally much greater in Rome itself than elsewhere, and owing to the turns of history advantage from them

133

fell mainly to the Papacy. And for the most part the Papacy did not fail the Western world; it faced its dangers and its duties boldly.

When Pope Leo died (November 10th, 461) he handed on to his successors some powers and policies which had gradually grown and were to grow much more in days to come. Already some rights of jurisdiction had been gained. The Council of Sardica (A.D. 343) by its Canons (III, IV, V) had given a right of appeal to the Bishop of Rome if a Bishop were deposed by a local council,[1] as might happen in a time of great ecclesiastical trouble with many contested sees. The Bishop of Rome was to name judges to try the case locally, but this provision was not always followed and appeals were sometimes tried at Rome. There had been a few isolated and natural appeals to the one Apostolic See of the West, but these, as Leclercq says, only prove the prestige of the Roman Church in communities far away, not the existence or exercise of a right of appeal.[2] But the State was interested in furthering the unity and peace of the Church, and the Church itself sought its help. Later on Valentinian I, about A.D. 367, set up an appeal to Rome by a law, the words of which are lost. His son Gratian was asked afterwards by a Roman synod (A.D. 378)[3] to give the support of the State for enforcing its decisions about discipline. The resulting rescript laid down that: were a Bishop deposed by Damasus the Pope, acting with other Bishops, or by a Council, the civil officers were to force his appearance before the episcopal court which had tried him, either at Rome or locally. In the more distant regions Bishops were to appear before their Metropolitans and the Metropolitans themselves if accused to be tried at

---

[1] Duchesne, *Histoire Ancienne de l'Église*, ii. 215 *seq*. (Eng. trans. 171 *seq*.); Hefele-Leclercq, [*Histoire des Conciles*], i. 737.

[2] Hefele-Leclercq, ii. 819–20 (note).

[3] The date is disputed: some give 380, some 382. See Puller, *Primitive Saints [and the See of Rome]*, p. 510 *seq*.; Hefele-Leclercq, ii. 55 (note).

Rome or locally by judges appointed by the Pope. If any unfairness by a Metropolitan or other Bishops was alleged, an appeal might be made to the Pope or to a council of neighbouring Bishops. In these provisions we may note the distinction implicitly drawn between the distant Bishops and those of the Suburbicarian dioceses. An authority over the latter had been recognised by the Sixth Canon of Nicaea.[1] The sphere of this authority covered South Italy, Sardinia and Corsica; it was akin to the jurisdiction of the Bishops of Alexandria and Antioch in large areas around their sees. But there was no fixed conciliar organisation with it as there was in North Africa and Egypt, and, as Duchesne put it: "It was only occasionally that Bishops who were strangers to the Suburbicarian province were present at Roman councils. Then there was no real influence upon the choice of Bishops, no regular means of putting oneself into relation with them; the superior government of the Pope was not really organised. When he was asked for advice he gave it; he sent some decretal letter, appropriate to the circumstance. Did persons arrive with complaints, he listened to them; and if it seemed opportune, he intervened in their business."[2] But we cannot as yet speak of a Patriarchate of the West, such as those found commonly in the East, although the imperial legislation had laid its foundation. In North Africa, however, there was a real Patriarchate; St. Cyprian systematised

---

[1] For the territorial extent of this power see Hefele-Leclercq, i. 563 seq., and Bright, [Notes on the Canons of the first four General Councils] (Oxford, 1882), p. 20. Rufinus, Hist. Bk. i. cvi, is the primary authority. For the chief canons and many important extracts, see Kidd, Documents Illustrative of the History of the Church (i. to A.D. 313; ii. to 461), S.P.C.K.

[2] Duchesne, Histoire, iii. 463—speaking of the fifth century. The three books of Mgr. Batiffol, L'Église naissante, La Paix Constantinienne, La Siège Apostolique, tracing the growth of Catholicism, and also of papal supremacy, are valuable and useful, even if all of his conclusions are not accepted.

its councils and so did much to start Canon Law in its long growth in Europe as a whole.

We thus see elements which, if made coherent, might become a solid system of ecclesiastical rule. But there is little apparent consciousness on the part of the early Popes of such a scheme. Not until the days of Damasus (A.D. 366–84) do we find something of the kind, and his Papacy has well been called "the period of the first definite self-expression of the Papacy."[1] It only needed that deliberate policy or statesmanlike power should weld these elements together.

But no Pope could of himself do everything that these beginnings seemed to foreshadow. The associations of the Empire had, however, pointed out one peculiar field of activity and a way of discharging the spiritual duties belonging to the Apostolic See. Roman ties with Gaul were many, and there some great cities had great sees with old traditions of their own. The ties with Rome were strong and were easy to make stronger. In one other direction the Papacy had found a platform from which it could, for other reasons, help to keep and quicken Catholic unity. The civil "Diocese" of Pannonia with its seven provinces touched both the Eastern and Western Empires, and soon became the playground of invading and conquering barbarians. In Noricum and Pannonia the churches kept touch with the Western Church as their civil organisation did with the Western Empire, and did this through the See of Aquileia, which was specially bound up with Milan. Dalmatia, however, looked to Rome. Under both Damasus and Zosimus, the Bishops of Salona, its metropolis, found help at need in papal intervention and sometimes came in for rebukes. Eastern Illyricum ecclesiastically looked to the

---

[1] *Camb. Med. Hist.* i. 171 (by the late Prof. C. H. Turner); Duchesne, *Hist.* ii. 460, on Damasus; Erich Caspar, *Geschichte Papsttums* (Tübingen, 1930), i. 261, is very good on the Pontificate of Damasus being more important than that of Siricius.

older Rome, although its political affinity was with the East. And so it was natural that Pope Siricius should delegate his power to the Bishop of Thessalonica as his Vicar (A.D. 383). But the political power of the Eastern Emperors and the rising ecclesiastical ambitions of Constantinople made this Vicariate a somewhat fitful and delicate growth, more of a memory than a solid fact.

It was otherwise with another more important Vicariate in Gaul, for there both political and ecclesiastical paths led to Rome. Zosimus (417–18) not only gave Patroclus, the Bishop of Arles, an enlarged jurisdiction as Metropolitan, trespassing on the old rights of Vienne, Narbonne and Marseilles, but also made him Papal Vicar over all Gaul.[1] However, not even the new invocation of St. Trophimus as founder of the see of Arles made this departure popular; many later changes came after protests and troubles, and at length (A.D. 445) Leo the Great came into strife with the Bishop, Hilary, through local discontent due to Hilary's dealings with other Gallic sees, and the Bishop of Vienne was made Metropolitan of the province instead. It was now that the Pope gained from Valentinian III a rescript repeating much of Gratian's but more precise in its terms and destined to better preservation.[2]   (445 A.D.)

Even apart from his personal greatness, Leo I was a model Bishop of his see. In the wider world he gave to Rome, or perhaps it might rather be said exalted, its reputation for orthodoxy. But his theological activities also deepened the growing gulf between East and West, and in the East there were many who thought, as Duchesne points out, that Cyril had been sacrificed for Leo. But it was a comparatively easy task for a great man with a wide

[1] Duchesne, *Fastes Épiscopaux de l'ancienne Gaule,* 84 *seq.*
[2] For the history, Kidd, *History of the Church to 461,* iii. 356 *seq.*; Duchesne, *Hist.* iii. 409 *seq.*; the rescript in C. Mirbt, [*Quellen zur Geschichte des Papsttums und des Römischen Katholizisimus*] (4th ed. Tübingen, 1924), 76. On 75 we have a letter of Pope Leo about the vicariate at Thessalonica.

vision to mould the floating elements of papal power into a coherent whole, and this is what Leo did.[1]

Bound up with Leo's regard for the unity of the Church was his use of vicars and (what was really his work) the introduction of Metropolitans into the West. Up to his reign, Metropolitans, found everywhere in the East, were far less common in the West, and he connected them with his Vicariates, trying to group them under the higher officers. More significant still, he brought the whole scheme to a head in his assertion of the special authority of St. Peter.[2] This authority was handed down to the holders of his see of Rome: he went a little beyond his predecessor Innocent I, who wrote something of the same to Victricius of Rouen, stressing the Canons of Sardica.[3] The assertion of Roman power now became part of the essential rivalry with Constantinople, and in this connexion use could be made of the pseudo-Clementine literature in which Alexandria and Antioch appear as secondary sees of St. Peter. As such they had a past greatness which put the newer Constantinople in the shade.[4] And Rome itself now came into rivalry with the new imperial city. The Pope was the natural spokesman for the West against the East; he often acted as such, and this increased his dignity and power.

There was a unity of the whole Roman world, expressed with a majesty able to overawe the barbarian invaders. But there was also an almost equally vivid unity of the Christian Church, quickened by contact with heathenism. And these two were joined together when Pope Leo faced the

[1] Ch. xi. and xii. in Erich Caspar's new volume *Papsttum*, i. deal with Leo. Specially noteworthy is the part 455 *seq.* on Leo and the unity of the Church.

[2] The most typical of his statements are conveniently given in Mirbt, 174 *seq.*

[3] See Mirbt, 62.

[4] On this see Caspar, *Papsttum*, i. 248 *seq.* Caspar's massive work (unhappily stopped by his lamented death) is meant to be a history of the idea of the Papacy, and it has thus special importance.

barbarians. The city of Rome was the very centre and symbol of the political unity. And at Rome, where the temples stood, deserted and unused, Christianity was supreme. The resulting state of feeling is well described by an older writer, who, after speaking of "the awful authority and dignity of St. Peter's chair," goes on to point out "the vast interest which every section of the Western or Latin Church felt in maintaining the integrity and securing the support of the great metropolitan and government-church," and "of the sense of the necessity of some central referee whose award should command the executive intervention of the State. Politically considered, this is the true key to the secret of the power of Rome. In some shape or other, every contest about jurisdiction, rank, territorial limits or authority between the higher orders of the hierarchy was sure to find its way to Rome. The civil government naturally leaned to a system of ecclesiastical policy most in harmony with those of the State; and thus at the court the Bishop of Rome came to represent the Church of the Empire and the religion of the Emperor. It was always most convenient to treat with him in the name of the whole." Thus there was "formed a spiritual monarchy in strict analogy to the state practice of the empire."[1]

A development can be traced between the view and assertion of Roman primacy from Innocent I (A.D. 401–17) to Leo I (A.D. 440–61). Innocent asserted strongly the power of the Apostolic See to give judgment in cases of complaints, and he founded this assertion on the Canon of Nicaea: but this was a confusion with the Sardican Canon

[1] T. Greenwood [*Cathedra Petri*, 6 vols. London, 1856 onwards], i. 291–2. This is a neglected but excellent, well-informed and judicious work, by an able scholar and lawyer; it may be classed as sometimes anti-papal, but it is always fair to individual Popes and it uses original authorities copiously and with judgement. It is always useful, if in some respects old-fashioned owing to citations of older editions of works now reprinted with better texts. There is a useful note on the earliest Decretals and their collections in Duchesne, *Hist.* iii. 21.

already mentioned. The East had for Nicaea (Canon VI) its original Greek; the West, most probably in good faith, had its altered Latin versions, incorporating in the text the heading current at Rome: "The Roman Church always held the supremacy." Documentary evidence goes against this form, but it was an anticipation of the growth which the Western Church was to pass through, and Western ecclesiastics acted as if it were true.[1] Other texts had histories much the same; the temporal dominion, even the ecclesiastical power, of the Popes owed much to the forged Donation of Constantine and the earlier *Actus Silvestri*.[2] Victricius of Rouen wrote to Innocent asking for advice on various points of discipline. The Pope gave the needed answers, doing so as he says "with the help of the holy apostle through whom both apostolate and episcopate in Christ had their beginning." The rules[3] were not, he said, new, but came from the traditions of the Apostles and Fathers. Greater causes are to be referred to Rome. The confusion between the Canons of Nicaea and Sardica arose most probably from collections of canons being made which began with those of Nicaea; there is no need to assume deliberate fraud. But, under Zosimus (A.D. 418), it caused

[1] On the text of the Nicaean Canon VI, see Hefele-Leclercq, i. 552, also Bright, *The Roman See in the Early Church*, p. 75, and the long note (utilising C. H. Turner's manuscript studies), 481 *seq.*; Kidd, *History*, ii. 46–7 is very clear and instructive.

[2] For the *Actus Silvestri*, see Döllinger, *Fables respecting the Popes of the Middle Ages*, 89; Langen, [*Geschichte der Römischen Kirche*], ii. 194–5, and Duchesne, *Liber Pontificalis*, i., cxi. The story that the leper Constantine was baptised by Pope Silvester at Rome was Eastern in origin and was inserted in the decretal *de libris recipiendis et non recipiendis* of Pope Gelasius, probably soon after his time. The most effective forgeries were not of Roman origin any more than were the *False Decretals*.

[3] Innocent gave something of the same guidance to Exuperius of Toulouse a year later. The history is given well in Kidd's *History*, iii. 6 *seq.*; Langen, ii. 11 *seq*. The most important words of Innocent are quoted in Mirbt, 76.

a discussion with the Church of North Africa, which was better informed than Rome about the legislation of Nicaea and knew little of the purely Western Sardica.[1] Apiarius, a priest of Sicca, had been rightly deposed and excommunicated by his Bishop Urban; he appealed to Zosimus, who reinstated him and sent him back with three papal legates, Faustinus, Bishop of Potentia, and two others. African synods questioned not only the papal reference to the supposed Nicaean Canons, but also the Pope's right to intervene: it may be taken that they repudiated the right of superintendence claimed by Zosimus.

One claim made by Innocent I was destined to be firmly built up into a tradition; that Rome was the founder of Christianity in the West. Writing to his suffragan Decentius of Gubbio (A.D. 416) he said that in "all Italy, Gaul, Spain, Africa and the adjacent islands no one has founded Churches except those whom the venerable Apostle Peter or his successors had set up."[2] So he claims they ought to follow what the Roman Church observes, from which Church without doubt they had their origin.

[1] See Kidd, *History*, iii. 162 *seq.*; Langen, i. 760 *seq.*, 796 *seq.*; Greenwood, i. 299 *seq.*; F. W. Puller, *Primitive Saints [and the See of Rome]* (a learned and accurate work) (London, 1900), 183 *seq.* For the important Canons of Sardica, Duchesne, *Hist.* ii. 171 *seq.*; Hefele-Leclercq, i. 737 *seq.*, and on the ecumenicity of the Council (which must be denied), 819 *seq.* Also C. H. Turner in *Journal of Theological Studies*, 1902, 970–97. Prof. Turner's Birkbeck Lectures at Trinity College on Early Western Canon Law are unhappily not yet in print. P. Fournier and Le Bras' [*Histoire des Collections Canoniques en occident*, i. and ii. (Paris 1931–2)], covers the ground.

[2] Ep. 25, Migne, *P.L.* xx. Harnack, *Mission and Expansion of Christianity [in the first three centuries]* does not consider Rome most active in missions; he questions its claim to have brought Christianity to North Africa, which for myself I should admit; he sees evidence only for a connexion of this kind with Edessa, to which place he holds the story of King Lucius to apply (see *Camb. Med. Hist.*, ii. 496 and 510). But the claim as made by Innocent was later on more or less taken for granted in the West. Harnack, however, does not consider it was historically true.

Church historians, as a rule, treat the early history of Canon Law as an illustration of the general history.[1] The late Prof. C. H. Turner in his *Studies* and in his chapter (i. c. vi.) in the *Cambridge Medieval History* indicated another way. It is much more a needed preliminary study. The early growth of Canon Law is really the fundamental process of the history. While I was writing this article there came into my hands, most usefully but too late for full systematic use, a book of the first importance, P. Fournier and Gabriel Le Bras, *Histoire des Collections Canoniques en occident depuis les Fausses Décrétales jusqu'à Décret de Gratian* (Paris, 1931). It has a full and luminous Introduction, which justifies the view I wish to give; that such a study is the key to the main lines of ecclesiastical history. The process of canonical history partly followed but also partly caused the constitutional growth of the Church. To begin with, we have collections separately gathered together in the great Churches, compiled for reference and convenient use. The existence at Rome of an old-established and trained administrative body naturally made a collection there peculiarly useful, and it was also frequently used. Such collections were gathered together in the fourth and fifth centuries, appearing at Rome during "the period of brilliant activity, beginning with Gelasius (492) and ending with Hormisdas (523)." Then we come to an age of national diversities in which, while the East and Italy devote themselves mainly to theology, the loosely connected Churches in Gaul put together collections made

---

[1] For the Canons of Nicaea, see Hefele-Leclercq (text and commentary), 503 *seq.*, their text 528 *seq.* There is a discussion of the question whether Sardica was ecumenical or not, 819 *seq.* For the question of the mingled Canons of Nicaea and Sardica, i. 464 *seq.*, and for the appeals to Rome, ii. 196. The Council of Constantinople (the Second Ecumenical) by its Canon III gave a place of honour next to Rome to Constantinople as the new Rome. There were many spurious Canons of Nicaea in circulation. There is a slight but useful book [*Les Sources du Droit Ecclesiastique*] by E. Cimetier (Paris *n.d.*).

up of earlier general canons and decrees of local councils; the Celtic Churches developed their Penitential codes (of which those important for England can be found in Haddan and Stubbs): the Spanish Church, more centralised and with a significant history, formed its own unique collection founded on the general councils and its own local councils, especially those of Toledo, which form a long sequence; it had behind it the conciliar ideals of St. Cyprian, and it also looked to the more present activities of Gaul. Martin, Metropolitan of Braga (*ob.* A.D. 580, born in Pannonia), had visited the East: he founded the monastery of Dumio near Braga, and was for the clergy of Galicia a teacher much like the Venerable Bede in the same fields of varied study, liturgic, catechetical and chronological. In his time two councils (561 and 572) impressed his influence upon the Spanish Church, and his canonical collection (the Capitula Martini), which included some new canons of the day from many places, summed up his work of reformation and order.[1]

But Gaul of the Franks was a prey to disorder, and this, working along with the inherited idea of the unity of the Church expressed by the Episcopate, forced the local Church to turn to discipline. Hence came some activity in councils such as those of Mâcon (581 and 585). And in the same way, with the still effective memories of Roman civilisation and Roman rule, the Church and its Bishops naturally looked to Rome for guidance and for systematic help.[2] Innocent I had said that churches ought to follow their founder the

---

[1] Fournier and Le Bras, *Collections*, 65–6; Duchesne, *L'Église au VIe siècle*, 564 *seq.* Fournier suggests that Martin forged some canons himself, while Duchesne gives a high character to him: an odd contradiction. See also Cimetier, 24.

[2] Ep. 25 in Migne, *P.L.* xx. 551–61; the most important part in Mirbt, 63. See Kidd, *History*, iii. 8 *seq.* Also Harnack, *Mission and Expansion*, i. 485, on the primacy of Rome; this he considers it had gained by the end of the first century, being the Church of the metropolis, also of St. Peter and St. Paul, as the Church which had done most for the catholicity and unity of the Church, and also by its generosity. But see p. 142, *note* 1, above.

Roman Church, a claim which was now oftener made and was more widely accepted, and the Frankish Church was now developing this view, doing so even retrospectively.

The position claimed by Innocent may, as I take it, be summarised thus: he asserted the Petrine origin of his see which gave it special importance and also responsibility. But this was part of the general episcopal inheritance; he built much on the conciliar decrees[1] and the imperial edicts; indeed there were occasional threats of imperial force, as in the case of Antony, Bishop of Fussala in North Africa,[2] and of Celidonius of Besançon, who, when condemned by Hilary of Arles, appealed to Leo the Great.

And there should be noted the appeal to the spiritual help of St. Peter, given to the Popes. Siricius had spoken of this almost mystical unity with St. Peter in the first(?) Decretal to Himerius, Bishop of Terragona (A.D. 385): "We bear the burdens of all who are heavily laden; or rather the blessed Apostle Peter bears them in us; for he, as we trust in all things, protects and defends us who are the heirs of his government."[3] Later Popes did the same, and in the eleventh century Gregory VII felt and spoke the same. More modern Popes have done so too.

When we come to Leo I we have a great ruler, fitted for his post by theology and knowledge of affairs, with a true vision of the post which God had called him to hold, and

---

[1] Although separation from the East was always growing, Eastern Canons were largely followed and quoted. Thus Zacharias (c. 747) quotes Canon X of Antioch (A.D. 741) at length in a letter to the Franks. See Dümmler, *M.G.H.*, iii. 481 (Epistles of St. Boniface and Lull). The influence of Eastern Canons, for instance, on the history of *chorepiscopi*, e.g. in the West, was great. (See C. H. Turner, *Studies in Early Church History*, chs. i. and ii.; Hefele-Leclercq, ii. 1197; Frere, *Visitation Articles and Injunctions of the Period of the Reformation* (Alcuin Club), i. Introduction, 9 *seq.*; Thomassinus, *Vetus et Nova Ecclesiae Disciplina*, pt. i., lib. i. ch. xxvii. (i.e. i. 91 *seq.* ed. 1691).)

[2] See Kidd, *History*, iii. 168.

[3] The decretal in Mirbt, 58. See Puller, *Primitive Saints*, 181 *seq.*

with a sense of his own real capacity to meet its demands.[1] Year by year, on the anniversary of his consecration (Michaelmas, A.D. 440), he preached on the duties of his office, with no feigned humility but with a deep understanding of all it meant. Such a balance of duty and power is only possible to the greatest of men. Starting with the vision of St. Peter as Innocent had seen it, Leo grows more and more into a sense of his right to rule derived from the Apostle; he begins with St. Peter and as years heap up he ends with himself. "If the other apostles had anything in common with St. Peter, their powers were only handed down to them through him." In the see of St. Peter "there lives on his power and the excellence of his authority." Peter was the mediator between Christ and the other Apostles, the channel of priestly grace, and all this, through his continued life, as it were, in his special See, comes to his successors in it.[2]

The discussion for us of all these matters often verges on controversy. But it is the task of historians to depict facts and things as they really were; as in ordinary life we come across people with whom we do not agree but whose reasons for their actions we can understand, so too in the history of the past. It is our business to try to understand, but never to distort, either it or the men within it.[3]

For papal jurisdiction Leo's dealings with Gaul need most notice. Trouble arose early in his reign (A.D. 444). Zosimus, as already said, had raised the ecclesiastical power

[1] There is an excellent page in Kidd, *History*, iii. 279. Bright, *Age of the Fathers* (ii. 413) aptly applies to him the Aristotelian definition: "a high-spirited man, who thinks himself worthy of great things, and in truth is worthy of them."

[2] The idea is akin to the legal conception of a universal successor, so familiar in the very home of Roman Law. But, of course, it was spiritualised.

[3] The late Bishop Gore's *Leo the Great* seems to me sympathetic and fair. He recognises where controversy impinges on history, and notes this: for controversy and history see N. Baynes's review of Caspar's *Papsttum* in *Eng. Hist. Rev.*, no. 186, 293.

of Arles. Its Bishop Patroclus thought that its ecclesiastical rank ought to match its civil importance. Zosimus made Patroclus become not only Metropolitan Archbishop of Arles with jurisdiction over Viennensis, Narbonensis I and II, and Alpes Maritima, but also papal Vicar for the whole of Gaul. Rome had always maintained, in opposition to the East, that ecclesiastical divisions arose from ecclesiastical traditions. So appeal was made to the story that the see of Arles had been founded by Trophimus the friend of St. Paul, who had come thither as a missionary from Rome. In this way local traditions, fondly cherished, now reinforced the Roman claims. In the sixth century Arles was a seat of canonical activity, favoured by the rich archives there: the compilations were mostly preceded by lists of Popes, and there was a wish to harmonise Gallic Church Law with Roman. Much was due to Cæsarius (503–543) to whom "il faut attribuer l'ascendant qui prit alors Rome sur la Gaule et de l'intervention de Rome naquirent chez nous les idées ultramontanes de cette époque.[1]

Up to this time the Church in Gaul had little organisation, although its prelates had often met in councils; so now a new period, not altogether happy at first, began for it. The sees of Vienne, Narbonne and Marseilles, felt their old existing rights in jeopardy. The Vicariate came to little, and Marseilles for the province of Narbonensis II repudiated the rival see. This was the state of affairs when the saintly Hilary (A.D. 429) from the great school of Lérins, which had already given its founder, his uncle Honoratus, to Arles as Archbishop, came to succeed his relative. Not only as a preacher (he was wont to preach sometimes for four hours on fast days) but as an evangelist

---

[1] *St. Cesaire* par l'Abbé Chaillan (Paris, 1912): Fournier and Le Bras, 27–29: C. H. Turner in *J.T.S.*, xvii. 236 *seq.* The work of the late J. Haller (*Das Papsttum* I: Stuttgart, 1934) approaches the history almost solely from the side: of the invading races, and not from the local Roman early church side this impairs its value. It is strange that death should have dealt thus with two latest Papal histories.

on foot in the districts around, the new prelate fulfilled his office. Such zeal was not always popular, and over the case of Celidonius, Bishop of Besançon, trouble began. When Hilary was visiting his friend St. Germanus at Auxerre he learnt that Celidonius was an offender against Church discipline; before his ordination he had married a widow and also as judge he had tried capital cases. So Hilary and Germanus went to Besançon, held a council and deposed Celidonius. The reasons for doing so seem trivial to us, but Hilary and Germanus went by the rules of their day although the former had no jurisdiction over Besançon. The dispossessed Bishop went to Rome. Leo received him favourably and took up his cause.

Hilary felt that the independence of the Church in Gaul was threatened by disregard of its council. He journeyed to Rome on foot. The local council, he argued, had obeyed the law of Sardica by a local trial and no power could reverse the decision. Then he went back to his work, but Leo, with his view of the papal power, reinstated Celidonius; he condemned Hilary, declared him no longer Metropolitan and deposed him. The Pope now got from Valentinian III the Rescript of July 445, already mentioned. It was sent to Aetius (Master of the Soldiers); no Bishops in Gaul or elsewhere were to decide anything without the authority of the venerable Pope of the Eternal City, and whatever his authority should assert was to be the law for all. The prefect was to see that the papal jurisdiction was enforced, and any Bishop who disobeyed a summons to Rome was to be compelled by the secular authority to due obedience. Hilary took little notice, although he sent messengers to pacify Leo. He died out of communion with Rome, but Leo spoke of him as a man of holy memory, and such indeed he was. But the jurisdiction of Rome had now imperial power behind it.[1]

---

[1] The rescript in Mirbt, 76. Good accounts of the history in Kidd, *History*, iii. 356 *seq*. and Bright, *Age of the Fathers*, ii. 419 *seq*. Fleury,

In this high-handed and masterly way Leo brought together ideas and assumptions which before his day had been floating in the air. He had the instinct of organisation, and so in a day of disorder he made his city and his see a centre of the world. Before him the Papacy was, as it were, incoherent; after him it was definite, impressive and majestic.

The Papacy under him and afterwards came before the Christian world, and the possible converts of the new races, as the special guardian both of Christian doctrine and canonical discipline. That was now to be its field for work. This view of its office was founded on statements about the past which inevitably led to controversies even more vital to-day than they were then, and which embarrass the historian in his search for the truth about both men and things. The lines laid down by the great Pope were followed by his successors, for the most part lesser men, to whom he left the task of working his ideal into a living shape. Its growth is what we have to trace.

But after the reign of Leo the history is more that of a constitutional growth than one due to the impulses of particular Popes. That growth was sometimes retarded, sometimes quickened by the movements of the new peoples, their absorption into the massive Christian civilisation of the Church and their reaction against it. These two things were always working under that complicated condition which was to form feudalism. It is naturally Gaul (now becoming Francia) and Germany which most concern us.

Among the Popes who need special notice Gelasius I (A.D. 492–6) comes first. His statement of the two governing powers, the sacerdotal and the temporal, is often mentioned;

Histoire du Christianisme, Bk. xxvii. chs. iv.–vi., is impartial, concise and sympathetic towards Hilary. The value of this great work is now not recognised as it should be, owing to suspicions of Gallicanism, and its age. But it can always be consulted with profit.

he made it in a letter to the Emperor Anastasius I.[1] Priests will have to give account for the souls of secular princes, and so their power stands highest; before them even kings must bend their heads. And among the sacerdotal principalities stands high above all that "which is acknowledged by the universal Church which was erected by the word of Christ Himself, that power which though often assailed by the kings of the world, still, like the rock on which it is founded, stands invincible and impregnable, the primacy of the Roman Church. By virtue of Christ's commission, the Roman pontiff becomes the gage and pledge to God for the soundness of the whole body of the Church; if the Apostolic See even in the smallest matter betray its trust or deal falsely with the Faith, the whole fabric of the Church, which is built upon the single foundation of St. Peter's confession, must be shaken to its base." Although written about the errors of Acacius of Constantinople, the statement is general, and well expresses the papal view. The immediate difficulties of Rome and Constantinople at the time of the Henotikon (A.D. 482) were very different, and there was mutual irritation between the sees.[2] Gelasius was not a Leo, but he was the heir of Leo's policy and conceptions and took his responsibilities strictly. This he showed in one special way. Writing to the Bishops of Lucania, Bruttium and Sicily, he laid it down that no Bishop was able to consecrate a church without papal permission. It was an effort, heroic but impossible, to deal with the threatening evil of churches founded by laymen, and too often regarded as their private property.[3]

It is well to pause a moment to note that along with this papal jurisdiction and world-wide business went the growth

[1] Given in Mirbt, 85. For a discussion, Greenwood, 52 *seq.*

[2] See Duchesne, *History* (Eng. trans.) iii. 346 *seq.*

[3] Ep. 14. See Paul Thomas, *Le droit de propriete des laïques sur les eglises et le patronage laïque au Moyen Age*, 15. Gelasius told Euphemius (Constantinople) that Popes were not bound like other bishops to notify their election: a new significant claim.

of a papal staff, the infant but future Chancery. Already the Popes had, of necessity, a staff of clerks on the model of imperial officers.[1] It is too early to speak of a Papal Chancery, just as it is too early to speak of the Western Canon Law; we are only at their beginning. But already the Papacy had its staff of secretaries and clerks, to multiply and be organised as intercourse and business grew. Already too there were collections of conciliar decrees in existence, beginning with those of Nicaea. To deal with the early history of the Papacy on its constitutional and legal side is impossible in a short sketch, but such an outlook must not be forgotten. For beneath the gradual and constant growth of papal power lay the appeal to these collections, sometimes misinterpreted, sometimes even vitiated by false versions.

All Bishops claimed a power derived from the Apostles. But the Bishop of Rome was marked apart both by his being the holder of the only Apostolic See in the West, and by the majesty of his city with its mingled traditions

[1] See R. L. Poole, *Lectures on the History of the Papal Chancery down to the time of Innocent III*, Cambridge, 1915; Lecture I, especially the Introduction. Also H. Bresslau, *Handbuch der Urkundlehre für Deutschland und Italien*, i. 2nd edn. Leipzig, 1912, the earlier chapters. For the constitutional history most useful works are: A. Werminghoff, *Verfassungsgeschichte der deutschen Kirche um Mittelalter*, latest edn. in *Grundriss der Geschichtswissenschaft* ed. Aloys Meister, Tübingen, 1907, and, of course, Hauck, *Kirchengeschichte Deutschlands*. For Gaul, P. Imbart de la Tour, *Les Élections Épiscopales [dans l'Église de France du IXᵉ au XIIᵉ siècle]* (Paris, 1891), which looks backward in its earlier chapters. The same writer's book *Les Paroisses rurales du IVᵉ au XIᵉ siècle* (Paris, 1900), covers the ground needed here; there was little organisation, and the election of bishops was the strongest link between the local churches.

For the general Church life, with its social background, we have: Sir S. Dill, *Roman Society in Gaul in the Merovingian Age* (London, 1926), following his earlier volume, *Roman Society in the Last Century of the Western Empire*. Also A. Marignan, *Études sur la Civilisation Française*: i. *La Société Mérovingienne*—the chapters on *La Société réligieuse*, (a) *Le Clergé seculier*, (b) *Le Clergé regulier* and (c) *La Vie réligieuse* and vol. ii. on *Saints*. Also Guizot, *History of Civilisation*, 3 vols. (trans. in Bohn's Library, 1880), a book old but invaluable.

of an imperial and a Christian past. In this troubled age many Bishops boldly faced the barbarian chiefs when most men's hearts were failing them for fear. The picture of Leo the Great proving his majesty before the invaders may have been the greatest instance, but among the Bishops there were many others, such as Epiphanius of Pavia and Anianus of Orleans. The horror of the time is revealed to us by writers like Salvian of Marseilles, who wrote his *De Gubernatione Dei* about A.D. 440, and Sidonius Apollinarius, who was a little younger. Christianity was a tonic for the hearts of men, and its Church, orderly in the awful days of disorder, was a refuge for their lives. Many Bishops proved their worth as leaders, and so their influence grew. Above them all so did the papal see. And we can understand how in those days of horror believers were drawn together and treasured the visions of unity which came to them out of the past. And for the Church, the order and brotherhood of the past was to be found mainly in the decisions of councils. In such an atmosphere, papal power grew greatly and guarded civilisation. What the Popes said or wrote should not be lightly dismissed as due to selfish pride or a wish for power. The multitude who listened were ready to obey.

We may pass quickly to Gregory the Great, who typified this Roman and Christian past. To the Church he brought a great gift in his personal humility, but he never hesitated to use his office as it had come down to him. His ideal of a Bishop's work needs no stressing, and Popes before him had in single cases dealt strongly with Bishops. Simplicius, a Pope of a rougher type, about A.D. 472, had deprived Gaudentius of Aufina (a see within his province) of his right to ordain, and confiscated three-quarters of his episcopal revenue. With the see of Ravenna outside his jurisdiction, he also came into conflict; John, the Archbishop, had compulsorily consecrated John, a canon of his Church, Bishop of Modena, a curious proceeding for which he might none the less claim patristic precedent. But Simplicius withdrew Modena from the control of Ravenna, claiming to be sole judge of the whole matter. Ravenna to a less degree than Constantinople was now an imperial capital, being the seat of the Exarch. This was one stage in a rivalry which was to last for centuries, and so the case came within the shelter of a constitutional dispute.

A more important step was taken when Simplicius (468–83) made Zeno, Bishop of Seville, his Vicar over the dioceses of Spain with a special charge to watch over the observance of canons, which was indeed what the Spanish Church needed. Since the heroic effort of the Council of Elvira, very early in the fourth century, to deal with a debased society and a semi-pagan tone of morals, little had been done. Heresy had been rampant and disorder flourished in the Church. The Vicariate did not perhaps come to much, but it did show that the papal eye was directed upon this outlying country, with its memories of Hosius the great ecclesiastical statesman of Nicaea and with its future of Moslem domination.[1]

Thus two conflicting principles or traditions were at work in the West; one was that all Bishops could claim a share in the power derived from the Apostles for directing the Church: the other was that the directing power lay with the see of Rome. The followers of each view saw the only hope for the disturbed world in the unity of the Church. But in a world and at a time so disordered it was difficult to keep this unity effective if the only means for securing it was for the Bishops to act together; some Bishops were negligent and some were bad; Gregory of Tours describes the evils of his day to be found among Gallic Bishops. On the other side the Popes sought to secure unity by the exercise of their own power and control of the episcopate. On the side of theory this meant the moulding into a more

[1] The Church of Spain ran a somewhat isolated course. See Duchesne, *L'Église au VIe siècle*, 548 *seq.* But its councils and canons were of importance,

compact form of the Roman tradition with its two elements, the scriptural basis of the Petrine texts,[1] and the appellate jurisdiction founded on imperial edicts and natural tendencies. The assertion of the first and the use of the second had each become more emphatic, and the resultant scheme of ecclesiastical control of the Western Church through its Bishops had now an easier way and worked more usefully in the disordered Western world. Rulers and powers of all kinds were living, as it were, from hand to mouth; the Papacy alone understood what it meant to do and knew how to do it with the means at its disposal.

The greatness of Gregory the Great was very different from that of Leo I. But although with very different backgrounds, in principle they were the same. Thus writing to Eulogius of Alexandria, with whom he had made friends at Constantinople, St. Gregory said about St. Peter: "Therefore, though there be many Apostles, yet, because of that sole principality which governs him, the See of the Prince of the Apostles is exalted above all, a See, which though set up in three different cities, is derived from him alone. For he did most highly of all exalt that see in which he took up his final abode and which he honoured by ending there his mortal course."[2] Thus we see at once a strong assertion of the papal position and combined with it one of the last flickerings on the papal side of the triple see of St. Peter (to be brought to light again much later by medieval enemies of the papacy); to which Leo the Great had alluded in his Chalcedonian letters of May 452.[3]

[1] These are St. Luke xxii. 31–2; St. Matthew xvi. 15–20; St. John xxi. 15–19; they began to be henceforth more appealed to. Bede, differing from St. Boniface and many later writers, says that what our Lord said to St. Peter he meant for all the disciples and not for him alone (see Migne, *P.L. col.* 222). Boniface marks a change in another way also. With him Rome becomes the "threshold (*limina*) of St.[r] Peter" not as before of St. Peter and St. Paul.

[2] *Ep. Greg. Magni*, lib. vii. 40, on Pelagius II, v. 18.

[3] See Kidd, *History*, iii. 337, for an account of Leo's action at this critical time.

In his discussion with Constantinople about the title of "ecumenical bishop" he says that his predecessor, Pelagius II, had of his own authority annulled all the acts of a council at Constantinople called by John the Faster. Without the authority and consent of the holy Apostolic See, no council, he asserted, had power or validity.

There is a curious letter from the Patriarch John II (519) sent with his signature to the *Formula* of Hormisdas (514–523), affirming his orthodoxy and admitting the Petrine claims. "For I hold the most holy churches of your elder and our new Rome to be one Church. I define that See of the Apostle St. Peter and this of the Imperial City to be one See."[1] Thus he "blunted the edge" of his submission.

In two directions Gregory gave a new turn to papal energies. Unable to go to England himself, by the mission of St. Augustine he brought the righteousness of God to a people that should be born. And secondly his love of the monasticism which he had himself embraced brought into the Church a new spirit of devotion. His interests in monasticism and in missions reveal his spirit.

In Gregory we can mark, I think, a new stage of papal supremacy. He was not a man to push claims which were doubted. He accepted them as handed down to him, a part of the inheritance of his See. On the side of the Eastern Empire and with the Exarchs at Ravenna he had continued troubles if not conflicts, though his loyalty was unquestioned. Troubles nearer at hand and more dangerous to Rome came again and again from the Lombards, and in Gaul the growing Frankish power had to be reckoned with. So politics pressed heavily on him. He panted (as he says) for the countenance of God, but clouds of secular business too often closed him in. His minute care for the vast but scattered

---

[1] English in Puller: *Primitive Saints*, 400. "A clever prologue": Hodgkin, *Italy and her invaders*, iii. 483, which summarises the situation. The *Formula*: Mirbt, 89. The letters in Migne, *P.L.* lxvi. 25–26, 43–45.

patrimony of his see has often been described, his justice and his care for charity were wonderful. But the confused state of Italy, the care of his city and his patrimony almost forced him to become a temporal ruler. He may be called (as many later Popes have been) the founder of the Papal States.

In England a Church arose which alone in the West was due to missionaries from Rome. And later we have the appeals of St. Wilfrid to Rome, coming from a Church up to then wisely, for the most part, left to control itself.

For these appeals we have two authorities; Bede, always accurate but here incomplete: Eddius, eager to extol his hero.[1] After 664, St. Chad was Bishop of York, St. Wilfrid of Ripon. When Archbishop Theodore objected to Chad's orders, Wilfrid took his place (669–677). But Theodore's scheme of new dioceses, and quarrels at Court, where Egfrid's bigamy was an offence, led to Wilfrid's withdrawal. Theodore consecrated Boro for York, Eata for Lindisfarne and Eadhaed for Lindsey: Wilfrid, unconsulted, had a grievance and appealed to Rome. A council (679) under Agatho decided the case on lines of justice, easy to trace for Roman experience. The three new Bishops were to be replaced by others, chosen by Wilfrid but consecrated by Theodore: everything was to be approved by a local synod. Wilfrid was restored to Ripon. After Aldfrid succeeded Egfrid, troubles arose again (691). Wilfrid probably left and acted as Bishop for Mercia (692–703): again he appealed to Rome. John VI (701–705) gave a "masterly" judgment,[2] recalling Agatho's decision, but as charges against Wilfrid had not

---

[1] *The Life of Bishop Wilfrid by Eddius Stephanus*, with text, translation and notes, ed. by Bertram Colgrave (Cambridge University Press, 1927), ch. xxiv. *seq.* Bede, Bk. iv., *passim* (in Plummer's ed.). Also Eadmer's *Vita Wilfridi Episcopi* in the Rolls Series (in *The Historians of the Church of York*, ed. by Raine), i. 161. See Bright, *Early English Church History*, ch. x.

[2] Dr. R. L. Poole, *St. Wilfrid and the See of Ripon*, *E.H.R.*, cxxxiii. *seq.*; the most decisive and clearest discussion of the matter.

been argued, the matter was referred to a local synod, and after Aldfrid's death peace among the Bishops came at a synod near the Nidd (*c.* 705–6) and Wilfrid once more ruled at Ripon until his death at 75 (12 Oct. 709). Happy in a monastery, joyously zealous in a mission, he was, perhaps, less at home in a diocese. He had a Northern jealousy of Theodore, although they became friends before his death: kings in that day were less righteous than of old but at Rome, whither tangled cases often came, there was justice and regard for local rights. His appeals were less of a crisis than Eddius and others since would have us think.

In his idea of the hierarchy and its foundation, Wilfrid belonged to the coming age. Here he rather differed from Bede, who held that what our Lord gave and said to the spokesman St. Peter, he spoke and gave to all the Apostles,[1] thus founding what may be called the oligarchy of Bishops, independent but joined symbolically through St. Peter and in the living unity of the Church into one coherent body for worship and for work. Wilfrid had even in boyhood and youth a wish to visit Rome,[2] and later days deepened the impression. We may remember that at the Synod of Whitby his appeal to the authority of St. Peter had turned the scale.

After St. Gregory's time we may consider the place of the Papacy fixed for the West. It was the special guardian of the unity and the discipline of the Church as expressed in its canons. And he had set his mark, that of his piety

---

[1] See my paper in "Anglican Communion" Murray, 1929, and Bede's Sermon XVI in Migne, *P.L.* vol. 94, col. 222. But Bede knew what in his day was the "modernist" view; in his work *The Six Ages of the World* (ed. by Smith) he quotes a statement from Paul the Deacon that the Emperor Phocas, in his strife with the Patriarch Cyriacus, decreed that "the Apostolic See of Rome was the head of all Churches, for that the Church of Constantinople had taken to itself the title of primate of all the churches." And we should not forget Bede's righteous and right veneration for St. Gregory the Great. I owe the reference to the *Six Ages* to Greenwood, ii. 239.

[2] Eddius, *Vita*, ch. iii. and Eadmer, *Vita*, ch. iv. *seq.*

and pastoral zeal, upon its work. In the *Liber Diurnus* the earlier parts reflect all this. The collection of formulae, copied and used at Rome, took its present shape between A.D. 685 and 751; some parts, Nos. 7–63, in the Vatican MS., belong to a seventh-century collection; Nos. 64–81 are a continuation down to about A.D. 700, and Nos. 82–99 were put together under Hadrian I (772–95).[1] For two and a half centuries it was in regular use; but it ceased to be so in the eleventh century. Letters modelled on its exemplars expressed what may be called the official spirit of Roman rule, even if its administration was reproached as it was by St. Boniface and earlier still by Northumbrian authorities in the affair of St. Wilfrid with too much of a mercenary inclination. But the formulae used in letters to Bishops are full of quotations from Gregory the Great, and thus we see how there was an attempt to rouse the whole episcopate, especially in Italy, to follow in his steps. This was to be done by strict observance of the canons. Thus, for instance, translations of Bishops were forbidden by Canon I of Sardica, and the first active interference of the Popes with the Frankish hierarchy takes place through papal consent being held necessary for translations. Otherwise episcopal elections are left to the local Churches and the share of the sovereigns in them is not questioned.[2]

For the Frankish Church the history of the growth of papal control over Metropolitans and Bishops is admirably traced by that accurate scholar Imbart de la Tour.[3] He deals with a later period, but sketches the earlier history.

---

[1] We have the edition by Sickel (1889) from the Vatican MS.; but E. de Rozière's edition (Paris, 1869) is very useful owing to its notes.

[2] Fr. Puller has calculated that between A.D. 688 and 1050 there were consecrated 376 bishops in England by action of the Chapters, the King and Witan, but without a trace of Papal interferences. I have verified this calculation.

[3] Imbart de la Tour, *Les Élections Épiscopales dans l'Église de France du IXe au XIIe siècle*. A masterly work.

The election was left to the locality, and by the primitive canons belonged to the clergy and people. Very soon the King or the great lords gained a place in it, and the chapter very naturally became the electing clergy. With this primitive rule the Papacy was content, and indeed strove to guard it. The same rule applied to Metropolitans, but here by the gift of the pall in the case of sees to which it was sent, there was a link with the Papacy. Until the eleventh century, however, there was no instance of an oath of fidelity to the Pope being taken by an Archbishop. After consecration the recipient of the pall sent to the Pope a profession of faith, which arose from the custom of a newly elected prelate announcing his election and his orthodoxy to his colleagues. But this had nothing of the nature of the oath of fidelity, which belongs to a later age.

The history of the pall (or pallium) I do not discuss here,[1] but it was to begin with a relic of St. Peter, consecrated by night on his tomb, and to be worn at Mass. It was meant to quicken in the prelate receiving it the sense of his pastoral care as inheriting its duties and its spirit from St. Peter. But later on it was to become more than a symbol and to be an instrument of power and control exercised over the Metropolitans. They were to be, as Cardinal Humbert puts it, the channels of papal power. This he expounded (c. 1057) in his *Libri Tres adversus simoniacos*.[2]

In the late Canon Lacey's *Roman Diary*,[3] he mentions a tea-table talk he overheard (none too well, unhappily) between Duchesne and Paul Fournier on the centralising movement of the ninth century. "Duchesne seemed to

---

[1] I have discussed this at some length in an essay, *Pope Gregory and the Hildebrandine Ideal*, in *Hildebrandine Essays*, 1932, Cambridge University Press, 45 *seq*. For details above, see Imbart de la Tour, *Les Élections Épiscopales*, 135, 137, 141.

[2] Reprinted in my *Hildebrandine Essays*, No. III, p. 47. The late J. Haller, in his *Das Papsttum*, I (Stuttgart, 1934), rightly takes Boniface as marking an epoch.

[3] London, 1910, 49.

think that it was forced on the Popes, Leo IV alone (or with Nicholas I) actually favouring it." When Canon Lacey brought the subject up again with Duchesne, the latter spoke of England under Dunstan as the chief field of this development, and also of St. Boniface compelling the Greek-born Popes of his day to take an interest in transalpine affairs.

Much, I think, confirms this view. I do not enter upon the ninth century, but the significant story of the Abbot Wala at the Field of Lies (A.D. 833) shows us a Pope (Gregory IV, 827–44) unwilling to decide a great issue because he was not sure of his right to do so. But he was convinced by being shown a collection of passages, canons and so on, which proved the Pope's prerogatives. So Frankish ecclesiastics went beyond the Pope in their doctrine of supremacy.[1]

But this conversation serves as a text with two heads for the development from Gregory the Great to Nicholas I; one head is the ecclesiastical atmosphere of Francia, and the other is the influence of St. Boniface. I take the latter first, for the stricter control over the Frankish Church more properly belongs to the ninth century, to that of Nicholas I and John VIII.

Much has been written about Winfrid (St. Boniface) (c. 687–754); patriotic Germans have later reproached his memory for subduing the German Church to the papacy, and the irritation often burst into protest; the medieval *Centum Gravamina* partly appeared in the much later *Punctation of Ems* (A.D. 1786).[2] And Boniface was often

---

[1] The story comes in Paschasius Radbert's *Life of Wale*, Bk. ii. ch. xiv. *seq.* Simson in his *Jahrbücher* doubted the story, but I should agree with Hauck and other later writers in believing it true. C. Rodenberg's dissertation *Vita Walae als historische Quelle* (Göttingen, 1887) is an excellent monograph and to my mind proves the truth. I give a fuller acount of it in my *Hildebrandine Essays*, 45 *seq.*

[2] I may refer to my account of St. Boniface in the *Camb. Med. Hist.*, ii. ch. xvi., 536 *seq.* There are two excellent Lives of him:

blamed for existing evils. Leaving aside his detailed life and work, a few points may be noted.

He was born near Crediton, and so belonged to the south; his outlook upon the Church was like that of Wilfrid rather than of Bede. Above all else he had the missionary longings which, largely in memory of St. Gregory, then filled the English Church. He had also a longing to visit Rome, pilgrimages to which were becoming commoner. Missionary method, too, was more studied in England than elsewhere, as we can see from the letter of Daniel of Winchester in answer to Boniface's prayer for advice. From the Pope he took commands, but from Daniel he got counsel. And English sympathy sustained him in his labours.

In 718 Winfrid visited Rome and there became a friend of the Pope, Gregory II (715–31). Then he worked in Thuringia and afterwards with Willibrord, also an Englishman working under papal sanction, in Frisia. Thence he went to Hesse, where his work was so successful that he felt a bishopric should be founded. Already his mind was bent on organisation. He sent a report to Rome and was called thither; on St. Andrew's day, 722, he was consecrated Bishop. At his consecration he took an oath, in form like that taken by the suburbicarian Bishops (those under the Pope as Metropolitan), but with one change; instead of the usual promise of fidelity to the Eastern Emperor, which was out of place for a missionary bishop in Germany, he promised to have no intercourse with bishops who did not obey the ancient institutes of the holy Fathers; he would, if strong enough, forbid them, and if this were fruitless,

---

Boniface of Crediton and his Companions, by the late Bishop G. F. Browne (S.P.C.K., 1910); *Saint Boniface*, by G. Kurth in the French Series, *Les Saints*; also Hauck, *Kirchengeschichte Deutschlands*, i. 456 *seq.* Letters between him and Daniel, Bishop of Winchester (in English) are in *The English Correspondence of St. Boniface*; *King's Classics* (London, 1911). My chapter, as above, has a full bibliography.

report them to the Apostolic See. In itself the oath was very little of a new departure; its likeness to that taken by the suffragan Bishops was the main thing; Boniface was being consecrated at Rome, and so naturally this oath (every Bishop took one) was like theirs. The new clause as to intercourse with erring Bishops was to guide him in his German mission, but it was sometimes hard to carry out.[1] The insertion of these words may have been due to the many talks with the Pope; joined to the memories of his sojourns in Rome they always had a great effect on him. He had instructions given him for the observance of canons which were rightly looked at as the great means for keeping the unity of the Church and a high standard of episcopal rule. His biographer, Willibald,[2] tells us of a little book given him "in which were written the most holy laws of the ecclesiastical constitutions as enacted in the pontifical synods." And for the papal see he had great reverence, as for St. Peter himself.

It is impossible to draw a strict line between ecclesiastical organisation and conciliar legislation; without the second, the first lost its spirit; without the first, the second lapsed. The two have their times of weakness and strength together.

[1] *Epp. S. Bonefatii*, No. 63—of a later date, after A.D. 742.
[2] In Levison's excellent edition *Vitae Sancti Bonifatii*, pp. 29–30. We should notice that Theodore at the Synod of Hertford (A.D. 672) had also laid before the bishops a like collection. See Haddan and Stubbs, iii. 118 *seq.*, for the similar council at Hatfield (A.D. 679); at the latter there were also adopted the Lateran Canons of Pope Martin I (October 649). See Bede, *H.E.* Bk. iv. ch. ii. Haddan and Stubbs, iii. 141 *seq.* For full accounts Bright, *Early Eng. Church,* for Hertford, 174 *seq.* and for Hatfield, 357 *seq.* In the earlier centuries a visit to Rome was described as one to the *Limina Apostolorum,* i.e. SS. Peter and Paul. But Boniface uses the term *Linmia S. Patri* twice. In the eighth century the usage varies, but later on *Limina S. Petri* becomes usual, although the other term appears in some forms of the oath taken by bishops to the Pope. See Ducange for *limina* (of a temple) *sub voce*. For fuller details see *Our Place in Christendom* (Longmans, 1916), 61–62. I correct the conciliar dates by R. L. Poole, in *J.T.S.*, xx. 27 and 34.

Of the important synods held by Boniface, and of his schemes of organisation under papal sanction, something has to be said later. But the correspondence between Boniface and Archbishop Cuthbert of Canterbury (A.D. 740–58) and the Council of Clovesho (September 747)[1] raise more than one question.

Boniface wrote to Cuthbert a letter obviously connected with the conciliar legislation: I think it preceded it, but perhaps it followed it. At the assembly two letters from Pope Zacharias (A.D. 741–52) were read in which he urged the need of strictly Christian lives for all. Neglect of this order or advice was threatened with excommunication. The letters were read with respect, but although their substance affected the details about morality of life, there is no mention of papal authority in the canons or in the constitutional enactments. Indeed, the canons seem to recognise no constitutional ecclesiastical authority beyond that of the Archbishop of Canterbury.[2] But stress is laid on the unity of the Church. The Homilies of St. Gregory are referred to as a guide for Bishops; in liturgy, litany, and music[3] the model of Rome was to be followed. But the records as they stand show us a national Church in full working order, part of the whole united Church in full

---

[1] *Epp. Bonefatii*, No. 78. Haddan and Stubbs, iii. 360 *seq.*; G. F. Browne, *Boniface of Credition*, 247 *seq.*; Stubbs, *Constit. Hist.*, I, ch. viii. gives the best background for the whole period; W. Hunt, *The English Church to the Norman Conquest* (Macmillan's Series, 1879).

[2] For the Canons (in English) see Johnson, *English Canons* (Oxford, 1850), 243 *seq.* In original Latin, Haddan and Stubbs, iii. 362 *seq.* For the Archbishop's jurisdiction Cannon XXV.

[3] St. Wilfrid had brought with him to Wearmouth John, Abbot of St. Martin's at Rome to interest his monks in psalmody, and he appeared as Papal Commissary at the Council of Hatfield to give teaching about the heresy of the Monothelites and Agatho's action against it. So John took up the musical work of James the Deacon of Paulinus, and Yorkshire owes the beginnings of its musical skill to these early teachers.

sympathy with Rome, but with no machinery for appeals
and so on, although these might, no doubt, be made without
any regular system by individuals, just as happened in the
case of Wilfrid.

But to return to the career of Boniface. After his consecration (A.D. 722) he went to work in Hesse, still regarding
himself as a Roman ecclesiastic, and then after much success
to Thuringia.

His work, both monastic and secular (in the ecclesiastical
sense), was so heavy that he wrote to the Pope (now Gregory
III, A.D. 731–41), complaining of his burden. The reply
was to make him Archbishop, so now not a mere isolated
worker he could call, almost command, helpers to his side.
In 738, he again visited Rome, and had a great reception.
On his return (739) to Bavaria, but now as a Roman
legate (*nostrum agentem vicem*, says the Pope), he held a
synod and created four dioceses, and later (741) divided and
organised sees in Hesse and Thuringia. All these measures
Zacharias, the new Pope (A.D. 741–57), confirmed. After
this Carloman asked him to come and reform the Church
in Austrasia, which greatly needed guidance. A council
(April 742) was the first step: under Boniface as a general
Metropolitan the work went on and was confirmed by
another synod, that of Estinnes (March 743), and then the
energetic and successful statesman was called to do the
same work for Neustria. Here again he began with a re-
organisation of the episcopate after a council for discussion.
Three archsees were planned for Rouen, Rheims and Sens;
for them Boniface asked palls, but a change was made,
and only Rouen received the pall.[1] Then (748) he was made
Archbishop and papal legate for both Austrasia and Neustria.
It was meant to do a great work for the Frankish Church,
such as Theodore of Tarsus and Canterbury had done for

---

[1] The reason for the change is doubtful. There was a correspondence
between the Pope and Boniface, and the latter's complaint of venality
at Rome was resented. All this I leave aside.

England. About the respective shares of the Papacy and Boniface in it, it is hard to decide. Probably the measures and the idea were the latter's, but Rome stood behind him. And a Church organised by Boniface, who was to have been Archbishop of Cologne, although in the end he went to Mayence, would stand differently towards Rome from one organised by Theodore. What was done was due to Boniface; from him the impulse came, and it seems as if Duchesne were right in thinking that it was rather he who led the Popes to action in the West, than they who sent him as a mere emissary; their approval went so far as to make him legate but really gave him a free hand. The constitution was due to Boniface, but what it was to grow into was to be decided by future history rather than by what the great missionary Saint did. The elements in the relation between the Pope and the German Church, which were afterwards objected to, were more the creation of time and its process rather than of Boniface, loyal Roman ecclesiastic though he was. It is as difficult permanently to combine centralisation and local liberty in the Church as in the State.

He himself received the pall (probably from Gregory III) when he was made Archbishop (732), ten years after his consecration. To this double link with Rome and St. Peter, he gave great significance. Writing to Cuthbert of Canterbury (A.D. 747) he says "a greater solicitude for His (God's) churches and a greater care for the people are incumbent upon us through our having received the pall, than upon other Bishops, because they care merely for their own parishes." The pall and his consecration oath, which was a personal tie, bound him to Rome, but the pall had for him, as he says here, a deep spiritual meaning, passing beyond any mere hierarchical ties. The unity of the Church built upon Christ was the greatest thing of all; he strove to do his part for it by forming in all his fields of work an ordered army of priests and bishops to teach and keep the Faith; over them were to be Metropolitans, and over them the Pope. This was with him more a spiritual than a legal or constitutional conception. There seems a vast difference between his ideal and that of Cardinal Humbert, three centuries later, to whom Metropolitans seemed mere channels of authority and grace which flowed from the papal power.

So this great missionary who, alike by his spirit and his organising power, left such a lasting mark upon the later world, may be looked at both as a spiritual force and as a maker of constitutions. In each of these he reaches the foremost rank, but he was more akin to St. Gregory the Great than to Gregory VII.

His earliest training was that of a monk, and from this there came, in that first bloom of monasticism at any rate, one characteristic which has been, so far as I know, noticed too slightly. In the life and training of monks, especially on the Benedictine model, obedience had a special and foremost place. Secular clergy were, of course, officially bound to obey the canons and be guided by their Bishop's command. But their life in a busy world with many calls opened many easy paths to disobedience and neglect. It was very different with a monk specially bound to obey and trained to do so: for him obedience was the foundation of life. So for St. Boniface, if I am not mistaken, the canons with their calls from the past to minute obedience had special force. His letter to Cuthbert shows his reverence for the canons which his Frankish councils had made, and the English canons, whether already passed or yet to be made, called for the same respect. This regard for conciliar legislation he impressed once for all upon his own particular churches. Did evils exist, it was for a council to stamp them out. Were better ways to be made easy or pointed out to all, it was for a council to show the way.

Nowhere did councils and papal authority work more closely together than in Frankish Gaul.[1] Appeals to Rome

---

[1] See Greenwood, ii. 137–8; Duchesne, *L'Église au VIe Siècle* (Paris, 1925), ch. xiii.; E. Caspar, *Papsttum*, I (Tübingen, 1930), 445.

for decisions, calls for advice or approval, had been commanded by imperial orders, and the traditions of Empire, as Carolings were quick to discover, lingered here when elsewhere they vanished. Gaul had been a special field for imperial Rome; it continued to be such for papal Rome. Collections of canons, the letters of Popes, all tell us the same. The Frankish Church was building up the edifice of papal supremacy more rapidly than did the Popes themselves.

Nor was there as yet any discordance between the authorities of Church and State. In the growth of Papal Jurisprudence, as I have tried to trace it, they had worked together, trying to keep the civilised world at one. Almost for the first time prophetic signs of future conflict came under Gelasius I (A.D. 492–6), whose letter to the Emperor Anastasius[1] is so often cited as speaking of the two swords, the two powers, united in Christ, although the superiority lay with the spiritual. This twofold division of powers was to rise to importance in later days, but as yet it only made a tiny ripple in the stream of history. St. Boniface had told Daniel of Winchester how, without the patronage of the Prince of the Franks, he found himself unable to rule the Church. And if, as Edmund Bishop insisted, Charlemagne was his own Minister of Public Worship (as in later days was Napoleon I, though with very different spirit and conception) there was, even under Gelasius, little thought of rivalry between Church and State. They grew in concord and they grew together, although there may have been a tiny rift to grow wider with time. We need to remember this when we look at the coronation on Christmas Day, 800. For Empire as for Church, Frankland was the forcing ground of institutions and ideas.

But if in Gaul, with its disorder on the one hand, its growth of Metropolitans under papal control and of an

---

[1] The significant passage is given in Mirbt, *Quellen*, 85. See Langen *Geschichte der Römischen Kirche* Bonn, 1885, ii. 168 *seq.*

episcopate, becoming so strong as to claim the guidance of affairs,[1] on the other hand, we best see the growth of papal jurisdiction, something of the same in conceptions and ideas can be seen elsewhere.

Thus in Africa,[2] now Catholic, not Arian, and made once more under the Enpire, we find a council of 217 Bishops at Carthage under Reparatus (A.D. 536) writing to the Pope John II for guidance as to the treatment of Arian churches and Bishops; they wished to deal with them charitably, but first they wanted to know what custom or authentic rule might have been adopted by the Roman Church upon the question. So being persuaded that the Pope, sitting in St. Peter's seat, and so entitled to all reverence, filled with all charity, ever speaking the truth in sincerity and doing nothing in the spirit of pride, with the true affection of their whole community, they turned to him for counsel and advice.

John II and his successor Agapetus (A.D. 535–6) replied. But, although dealing with the same matter and requests, there is a significant difference between the African and the papal way of looking at them. Agapetus expressed himself glad that they had not lost sight of the principality of the Apostolic See, and that as in duty bound thay had turned to that throne to which the power of the portals (*i.e.* of heaven and hell) had been entrusted. As Metropolitan,[3] Reparatus was told to carry out the papal decree so that no one should remain ignorant of the decision of the Apos-

---

[1] See the chapter by Prof. L. Halphen in *Camb. Med. Hist.*, iii. 445 *seq.* This was the episcopal interpretation of the unity I speak of above.

[2] Greenwood, ii. 138 *seq.*; Richard, *Analyse des Conciles*, i. 524–5; Langen, 325 *seq.*; also Duchesne, *L'Église au VIᵉ Siècle*, 540 *seq.*; Hefele-Leclercq, ii. 1136 *seq.*, correcting the date 534 usually given; Migne, *P.L.* lxvi. cols. 25–26 and 43–45.

[3] There is a useful passage on the North African Church with its Patriarchate (or quasipatriarchate) and its councils in Puller, *Orders and Jurisdiction* (London, 1925), 220.

tolic See upon consideration of the canons. The Africans, disordered by heresies and long persecutions, sought advice from the more settled capital, but Agapetus, stressing the *principalitatem Apostolicæ sedis* over Metropolitans, spoke with authority.

We have thus in the sixth century a theory of Papal Jurisdiction, clear in its expression from time to time and hinting at more than had become effective in fact; some powers had been occasionally claimed, such as control of councils and need of papal consent for their validity, of papal power exercised everywhere through Vicars and Metropolitans under them. But most of these claims were as yet programmes for the future rather than actual fact. In its gift of the pall, however, there was a link in the growing chain of power to be drawn tighter as years passed on.

The East now, for the most part, stood aloof, but sometimes sought friendship if Emperor or Patriarch needed help. In the West, individual national Churches seemed to have different views of policies. The world was changing and confused; in some countries barbarian ignorance prevailed: in others primitive customs and ancient learning were treasured. Times and things were disordered, and Churches often at a loss. Everything seemed to turn on the forces which made for unity. Therefore much depended on the Papacy, much also depended upon the episcopate and upon its councils. This was a great responsibility for the Church: it called for the surrender of self and for a devoted service. History was to test all ranks of the clergy. It was theirs to keep the spiritual Temple in fit repair, with its servants on guard and its lamps alight. Only so could a world, old but new, be saved. It was a stringent test, which left no space for selfishness or sloth or sin.

INDEX

A

ACTON, LORD, 3, 11, 30, 92, 98
Actus Silvestri, 140
Address to the Nobility (Luther's), 113–114
Adrian VI, 32, 51, 55, 75, 76
Aeneas Sylvius (Pius II), 11, 18, 23, 56
Aetius, 147
Africa, N. Patriarchate, 135, 141, 167
Agapetus, Pope, 167–168
Aldus and the Aldine Press, 59, 63, 64, 67
Alexandria, 135, 138, 153
Antioch, 135, 138
Aquinas, St. Thomas, 27
Arians, 167
Augustine, St., 13, 29, 84, 102
Augustinian Friars, 10, 12, 19, 28, 56

B

Basle, 22, 44, 59, 68–9, 74, 82, 84, 85
Bede, 143, 155, 156, 160
Bessarion, 9
Beza, Theodore, 22, 56, 70
Boniface, St., 157, 159–166
Bossuet, 96, 122
Brandenburg (Prussia), 116, 121–126
Brethren of the Common Life, 10, 19, 52, 69, 87
Bucer, Martin, 29, 93, 100

C

Calvin, 24, 26, 30, 69, 70, 85, 108, 110, 119, 122
Cambridge, 67, 68, 84
Canon Law, 136, 142–143, 150
Capitula Martini, 143
Caraffa. *See* Paul IV.
Cardinal of Lorraine, 26
Centum Gravamina, 107, 159
Charlemagne, 166
Charles V, 26, 68, 83, 92, 102, 108
Cicero, 44, 47
Colet, 60, 66, 72, 115
Common Prayer, Book of, 122
Confession (Apology) of Augsburg, 29, 92, 110, 112
Constance, Council of, 32, 55
Constantinople, 9, 137, 138, 149, 153, 154
Contarini, 27, 28, 78
Cornelius Gerard, 11, 61
Counter-Reformation, 34, 35, 49, 72, 86, 116
Cranmer, 13, 70, 85, 92
Cyprian, St., 135, 143

D

Dalmatia, 136
Damasus, Pope, 134, 136
Denifle, 4, 12, 13, 19, 44, 98–102
Döllinger, 114–117
Donation of Constantine, 140
Duchesne, 135, 137, 158, 159–164

PRINTED IN GREAT BRITAIN BY RICHARD CLAY AND COMPANY, LTD.,
BUNGAY, SUFFOLK.